OCCASIONAL
P A P E R

Stray Dogs and Virtual Armies

Radicalization and Recruitment
to Jihadist Terrorism in the
United States Since 9/11

Brian Michael Jenkins

INVESTMENT IN PEOPLE AND IDEAS

This publication results from the RAND Corporation's Investment in People and Ideas program. Support for this program is provided, in part, by the generosity of RAND's donors and by the fees earned on client-funded research.

Library of Congress Cataloging-in-Publication Data is available for this publication

ISBN: 978-0-8330-5880-5

The RAND Corporation is a nonprofit institution that helps improve policy and decisionmaking through research and analysis. RAND's publications do not necessarily reflect the opinions of its research clients and sponsors.

RAND® is a registered trademark.

Published 2011 by the RAND Corporation
1776 Main Street, P.O. Box 2138, Santa Monica, CA 90407-2138
1200 South Hayes Street, Arlington, VA 22202-5050
4570 Fifth Avenue, Suite 600, Pittsburgh, PA 15213-2665
RAND URL: http://www.rand.org/
To order RAND documents or to obtain additional information, contact
Distribution Services: Telephone: (310) 451-7002;
Fax: (310) 451-6915; Email: order@rand.org

Preface

In 2010, Brian Michael Jenkins, Senior Adviser to the President of the RAND Corporation, examined the phenomenon of homegrown terrorism in the United States and suggested some strategies for changing the approach to fighting terrorism as terrorism itself changes. That work is documented in *Would-Be Warriors: Incidents of Jihadist Terrorist Radicalization in the United States Since September 11, 2001* (RAND Occasional Paper OP-292-RC, 2010).

As the nation observes the 10th anniversary of the 9/11 attacks, Americans are mindful of the terrorist threat and wondering where the nation stands. In this new paper, Jenkins revisits the topic of homegrown terrorism, expands on his remarks about the current environment and domestic counterterrorist strategy, and updates the numbers and case descriptions to include all of 2010. The discussion should be of particular interest to local, state, and federal law enforcement authorities.

This publication results from the RAND Corporation's Investment in People and Ideas program. Support for this program is provided, in part, by the generosity of RAND's donors and by the fees earned on client-funded research.

Contents

Summary

The evidence suggests that al Qaeda, although weakened, remains as intent as ever on its worldwide terrorist campaign. But it faces a more difficult and dangerous operating environment than it did 10 years ago and has necessarily changed its approach. Instead of conducting large-scale attacks, which are difficult to plan and implement in the glare of improved U.S. intelligence, al Qaeda seeks American homegrown recruits to implement a campaign of individual jihad and do-it-yourself terrorism.

How successful has al Qaeda been with this new approach in the years since 9/11? So far, the turnout is tiny. A total of 176 Americans have been indicted, arrested, or otherwise identified as jihadist terrorists or supporters since 9/11. The 176 individuals were involved in 82 cases, 20 of which were announced in 2010, as compared with 15 in 2009.

This analysis counts cases, plots, and individuals. A case represents the culmination of an investigation. It may involve a single individual or a group of persons charged with materially assisting or joining a jihadist terrorist group abroad or with plotting terrorist attacks in the United States. Plots comprise the subset of cases in which individuals or small groups were accused of planning terrorist attacks against targets in the United States. Obviously, these cause the greatest concern.

The number of cases and individuals involved in homegrown terrorism increased in 2009 and again in 2010, but counting cases turns out to be an imperfect way of measuring activity. In fact, fewer individuals were arrested or indicted in 2010 than in 2009, while the cases in both years reflect investigations of activity going back to the middle of the decade.

This paper examines the cases of homegrown terrorism from September 11, 2001, through 2010 and highlights lessons learned from those cases that suggest actions for the future.

Working alone or with others, so-called homegrown terrorists planned and in some cases implemented terrorist activities, contributed financial or other material support to others' terrorist activities, or became radicalized in the United States and then traveled to other countries to conduct terrorist activities directed against those countries or against the United States. They were "jihadists" in that they subscribed to al Qaeda's ideology of worldwide terrorism.

In the United States, to hold radical views is not a crime. The Constitution provides strong protection of individual beliefs and free speech. Only when these turn to criminal incitement and violent action or manifest intent to engage in violence is there cause for legal intervention—this is why analysts favor the complete phrase "radicalization *and* recruitment to terrorist violence." It is the second step that makes the first step a matter of concern.

The 82 cases since 9/11 involved 32 plots. Few of these 32 got much beyond the discussion stage. Only 10 developed anything resembling an operational plan that identified a specific target, developed the means of attack, and offered a sequence of steps to carry out the planned action. Of these, six were Federal Bureau of Investigation (FBI) stings. Only two individuals actually attempted to build devices on their own. One was arrested while doing so, and the other's device failed. The rest of the would-be terrorists only talked about bombs. In only two cases did jihadist terrorists actually succeed in killing someone, and both of these cases, which occurred in 2009, involved lone gunmen.

The recruits are generally young, although a bit older than the average American criminal offender. The overall average age of recruits is 32, and the median age is 27. The number with a high school education or less coincides roughly with the national average for men 25 and older. More jihadists started college than the national average (many attended local community colleges), but far fewer graduated, since many dropped out in their early twenties to join the jihadist campaign.

Arab and South Asian immigrant communities are statistically overrepresented in the small sample of recruits for whom we have information about national origin, and most are Muslim, but the numbers are still small: 176 terrorists out of an American Muslim population of several million comes to roughly 6 out of 100,000. Meanwhile, several thousand Muslim Americans serve in the U.S. armed forces. A mistrust of American Muslims by other Americans therefore seems misplaced.

Somalia merits special concern. Four of the 20 cases in 2010 involved recruiting or fundraising for the al-Shabaab group in Somalia, and four more involved individuals going or attempting to go to Somalia to join this group. A ninth case involved a Somali-American planning a terrorist attack in the United States. Overall, Somalis and Pakistanis are heavily represented among America's homegrown jihadists. In Europe, Somalis, Algerians, and Pakistanis predominate; all three countries are engaged in major internal conflicts, suggesting that local diaspora communities with links to war zones and struggling with assimilation are the most likely to produce homegrown terrorists.

Stray Dogs and Virtual Armies

Radicalization and recruitment to terrorism, in person or on the Internet, does not appear to be a community phenomenon; rather, it is an individual decision. In fact, a majority of the 82 cases described in this paper involve the actions of a single individual attempting to join a jihadist front abroad or plotting to carry out a terrorist attack in the United States. Analysts have tended to call such individuals "lone wolves," in my view, a romanticizing term that suggests a cunning and deadly predator. A few of those recorded here display this kind of lethal determination, but others, while still dangerous, skulk about, sniffing at violence, vocally aggressive but skittish without backup. "Stray dogs," not lone wolves, more accurately describes their behavior.

On the other hand, many conspirators were working for al Qaeda at the time of their arrest. Eight of the individuals were working with FBI or police informants or undercover agents whom they believed to be part of al Qaeda or some other jihadist group. They had connected with a group, but it wasn't the one they expected.

A Preventive Approach

Traditional law enforcement, in which authorities attempt to identify and apprehend a perpetrator *after* a crime has been committed, is inadequate to deal with terrorists who are determined to cause many deaths and great destruction and who may not care whether they themselves survive. Public safety demands a preventive approach—intervention *before* an attack occurs.

Prevention includes working closely with the communities from which terrorists emerge to elicit their cooperation—family and friends may dissuade would-be terrorists from taking action or alert the authorities to potential violence, and on occasion they have done so. Prevention also means working with these communities to help them assimilate, earn their trust, and prevent discrimination. At the same time, Muslim Americans must accept that while religion alone does not make the community a target of the state, neither does it provide immunity from legitimate intelligence and law enforcement investigations. Policing efforts aimed at enlisting community cooperation and intelligence efforts aimed at preventing and deterring terrorist activity that would endanger society and the Muslim communities themselves will continue.

One way of finding out who might be dangerous is to probe intentions with sting operations, which lubricate the suspect's decisionmaking. Instead of monitoring a subject for months, perhaps years, sting operations offer him the means to take action. Indeed, FBI sting operations have interrupted a substantial number of plots that may or may not have otherwise been successful. Stings will continue to be necessary, but they must be closely managed to preclude entrapment.

Since 9/11, al Qaeda has increasingly used the Internet to build an army of followers. Many of the terrorists identified in this paper began their journey on the Internet. However, al Qaeda has not yet managed to inspire many of its online followers to action. In the United States, its virtual army, with a few exceptions, has remained virtual.

Prevention will not always work. Al Qaeda remains a threat. More terrorist attempts will occur. In addition to traditional law enforcement, intelligence collection, and community policing, public reaction is an essential component of homeland defense. Needless alarm, exaggerated portrayals of the terrorist threat, unrealistic expectations of a risk-free society, and unreasonable demands for absolute protection will only encourage terrorists. Panic is the wrong message to send to America's terrorist foes. As long as America's psychological vulnerability is on display, jihadists will find inspiration. More recruitment and more terrorism will follow.

Acknowledgments

This paper has benefited greatly from formal reviews by Karen J. Greenberg, Executive Director, Center on Law and Security, NYU School of Law; and Jack Riley, RAND Corporation Vice President and Director of the RAND National Defense Research Institute. I am, however, solely responsible for the content and views expressed.

I also wish to thank Shelley Wiseman for her thoughtful questions and assistance in organizing the paper and Janet DeLand for her always skillful editing.

This continuing line of independent research would not be possible without the support of the RAND Corporation and its president, Jim Thomson.

Al Qaeda's Emphasis on Do-It-Yourself Terrorism

Years of unrelenting pressure on al Qaeda have degraded its operational capabilities, and improved intelligence has made the terrorists' operational environment more dangerous, yet there is no evidence that al Qaeda's determination to continue its terrorist campaign has diminished. As documents discovered at Osama bin Laden's compound in Pakistan indicate, the leader of al Qaeda spent his days exhorting his followers to attack the United States and suggesting ways they might do so. But he was communicating to a more decentralized enterprise, one far more dependent on its regional affiliates, like-minded allies, and above all, local recruits to plan and carry out attacks. Al Qaeda's terrorist campaign has evolved from centrally planned and directed large-scale attacks to a growing emphasis on individual jihad and do-it-yourself terrorism by homegrown extremists.

This paper examines the cases, individuals, and plots inspired by al Qaeda's ideology of global jihad, in which local attacks by homegrown terrorists have become a key component.

The analysis suggests that homegrown jihadists pose a terrorist threat, but thus far, despite al Qaeda's intensive online recruiting campaign, their numbers remain small, their determination limp, and their competence poor. Even the apparent uptick in arrests in 2009 and 2010 turns out upon close examination to be the culmination of investigations of activity in earlier years, the result of young Somali-Americans going off to fight Ethiopian invaders, and the honing of the Federal Bureau of Investigation's (FBI's) investigative techniques that have led to a number of stings. The increase is real, but it is gradual.

However, this is no reason for complacency: 2009 and 2010 witnessed the first terrorist attacks with fatalities in the United States since 9/11, both carried out by lone gunmen; the first actual attempted bombing that was not an FBI sting; and perhaps the most serious terrorist plot, the Zazi case. (Najibullah Zazi acquired the ingredients to make an explosive device, but U.S. authorities interrupted his scheme.) Time abroad appears to be very important in motivation and know-how, although Major Nidal Hasan had none when he killed 13 soldiers at Fort Hood, Texas. Amateurs can be lethal.

The level of threat could change if, for example, Somali-Americans serving with al-Shabaab in Somalia were able to slip back into the United States undetected and begin terrorist campaigns or if al Qaeda's exhortations to violence eventually began to show better returns among those already in the United States. Finally, although it has been successful thus far in interrupting terrorist plots, domestic intelligence collection still requires improvement in many aspects.

The Terrorists

Who's In and Who's Out?

The terrorist groups in this homegrown jihadist universe include al Qaeda and its regional affiliates, especially the increasingly important Yemen-based al Qaeda in the Arabian Peninsula, and allies such as al-Shabaab and two groups in Pakistan: Lashkar-e-Toiba and Tehrik-e-Taliban Pakistan. Not all of the cases discussed here can be directly connected to one of these groups, but all of them display evidence of jihadist radicalization.

However, not every Muslim with a gun should be labeled a jihadist, even when targets suggest political motives or personal prejudices. For example, Hesham Mohamed Hadayet, the Egyptian chauffeur who in 2002 opened fire on the El Al counter at Los Angeles International Airport, was not found to be connected to any terrorist organization or political cause. His assault may be described as a hate crime or an act of terrorism, but his chosen venue and target do not in themselves make him a jihadist. Neither were the sniper attacks in and around the District of Columbia carried out in 2002 by John Allen Muhammed and Lee Boyd Malvo acts of jihad. Muhammed's intent was to disguise the intended murder of his ex-wife with the killing of victims selected at random, although later, in prison, he scribbled an erratic screed about jihad.

This paper excludes cases connected with providing support to Hamas, Hezbollah, or other organizations that subscribe to radical Islamist political ideologies and employ terrorist tactics but are not considered part of the terrorist universe inspired by al Qaeda. These groups have engaged in illegal fundraising activities in the United States, but their leaders have not called for terrorist attacks on the American homeland as has al Qaeda.

In the cases considered here, Americans committed crimes as defined in various federal statutes. They provided material support to a designated jihadist terrorist group, joined or attempted to join one of the jihadist fronts abroad, or plotted to carry out terrorist attacks in the United States or elsewhere.

This analysis counts cases, plots, and individuals. A case represents the culmination of an investigation. It may involve a single individual or a group of persons charged with materially assisting or joining a jihadist terrorist group abroad or with plotting terrorist attacks in the United States. For reasons described later, however, cases can be a misleading measure of terrorist activity.

Plots comprise the subset of cases in which individuals or small groups were accused of planning terrorist attacks against U.S. targets. Obviously, these cause the greatest concern. The number of *individuals* identified each year provides a more accurate measure of the terrorist threat.

"Americans," in this study, include U.S.-born Americans, naturalized U.S. citizens, legal permanent residents, and others living in the United States legally or illegally. Individuals who were radicalized and recruited abroad and who then came to this country specifically to carry out terrorist attacks are not included. Therefore, the study excludes the 9/11 attackers, even though some of them had lived in the United States for months. It also excludes Richard Reid, the "shoe bomber," a Jamaican radicalized in the United Kingdom who attempted to sabotage an airliner bound to the United States from France; Umar Farouk Abdulmutallab, a Nigerian radicalized while living in the United Kingdom and Yemen who attempted to sabotage another airliner as it flew to Detroit; and Khalid Al-M Aldawsari, a Saudi college student who was arrested in Texas in February 2011 for attempted use of explosives. When Aldawsari arrived in the United States in 2008, he was already planning terrorist attacks.

The names of the individuals in these cases come from arrests or indictments for particular crimes. Others have identified themselves by their own deeds as jihadist terrorists, even though they may not have been indicted. For example, the case of Omar Hammami, a young American who went to Somalia in 2007 and began making propaganda videos for al-Shabaab, was listed in an earlier RAND report on radicalization[1] under the year 2007, although he was not indicted until 2010. Although never indicted, Shirwa Ahmed—the first American suicide bomber—who blew himself up in Puntland, Somalia, in 2008, is also included in the cases presented here.

The Numbers

All studies of radicalization have their own numbers. These vary depending on the time frame and the authors' criteria for inclusion, which easily can and should be explained. The differences are seldom significant. However defined, the total number of American jihadist terrorists is small. The only thing that could significantly change the total would be a subsequent revelation that many hundreds of suspects were secretly arrested.

Numbers of Cases of Terrorism in the United States

The number of homegrown jihadist terrorism cases each year since 9/11 is listed in the table below. The increase in the number of cases from 15 in 2009 to 20 in 2010 may be somewhat misleading, depending on how cases are aggregated.

Four of the 20 cases in 2010 involved recruiting or fundraising for the al-Shabaab group in Somalia, and four more involved individuals going or attempting to go to Somalia to join this group. There were 11 separate indictments in these eight cases. But the count of the cases can vary depending on whether arrests, indictments, and activities are clustered together and counted as one or are counted individually. The eight al-Shabaab cases could have been portrayed as five cases, resulting in a total of 17 cases in 2010 instead of 20.

Two of the eight cases included four related indictments of 14 persons connected with recruiting and fundraising for al-Shabaab. All of the indictments were issued by the U.S.

---

[1]   Brian Michael Jenkins, *Would-Be Warriors: Incidents of Jihadist Terrorist Radicalization in the United States Since September 11, 2001,* Santa Monica, Calif.: RAND Corporation, OP-292-RC, 2010.

**Cases of Homegrown Terrorism in the
United States, 9/11 Through 2010**

Year	Number of Cases
2002	6
2003	6
2004	11
2005	5
2006	9
2007	6
2008	4
2009	15
2010	20

Department of Justice on August 5, 2010. These indictments are presented in the chronology at the end of this paper as two separate cases, one involving recruiting and fundraising and another involving Americans who had already joined al-Shabaab in Somalia, but they could just as easily have been presented as one case. Similarly, in November 2010, seven people connected with fundraising for al-Shabaab were arrested in four cities. These are portrayed in the chronology as three separate clusters of cases, but they could just as easily have been portrayed as a single multicity investigation of terrorist fundraising. The remaining three cases involve arrests of individuals on their way to join al-Shabaab.

Regardless of exactly how the cases are counted, the total figures for 2009 and 2010 reflect a higher level of activity than that in 2002 through 2008, during which there was an annual average of six to seven cases involving an average of 15 persons. The apparent uptick first noted in 2009 therefore seems not merely to have been a spike but may signal a trend. More than three-quarters of the total number of American jihadists identified since 9/11 were identified in 2009 and 2010, although the numbers of cases and of individuals involved are still very small.

Even this apparent recent increase may be discounted by the fact that a number of the cases listed for 2010 reflect earlier activity. The example of Omar Hammami has already been mentioned. Jehad Sherwan Mostafa, who also was indicted in 2010, actually left the United States in 2005 and reportedly served with al-Shabaab in 2008 and 2009. Federal authorities indicted Wesam el-Hanafi and Sabirhan Hasanoff in 2010 for providing material support to al Qaeda, but their activities began in 2008. The indictments in the 2010 Somali recruiting case also reflect investigations of events that began in 2008. Nevertheless, we can confidently say that there has been an increase over the past several years.

In addition to the 2010 cases, 16 cases have been added to the list that appeared in the earlier RAND paper, which covered the period from 9/11 to the end of 2009.[2] The entire chronology of 82 cases is included in this paper.

---

[2]   Jenkins, 2010.

Numbers of Individual Homegrown Terrorists

The numbers of Americans who have been indicted, arrested, or otherwise identified as jihadist terrorists or their supporters since 9/11 are listed by year in the table below.

In six cases in 2010, individuals were charged with recruiting, raising funds, or providing other forms of material assistance to designated jihadist terrorist groups. In eight cases, individuals were charged with joining or attempting to join jihadist groups abroad. (In one of those eight cases, some individuals were acting as recruiters.) In the remaining cases, individuals who were inspired by jihadist propaganda discussed or planned to carry out terrorist attacks in the United States.

Seven of the individuals named as al-Shabaab recruits in 2010 had been named in indictments issued in 2009. Excluding these and Omar Hammami leaves 31 new jihadist terrorists and supporters identified in 2010, compared with 40 individuals identified in 2009.

**Individuals Involved in Homegrown Terrorism
in the United States, 9/11 Through 2010**

Year	Number of Individuals
2002	18
2003	18
2004	16
2005	12
2006	26
2007	11
2008	4
2009	40
2010	31

In addition to the 176 who were arrested or indicted for terrorist activity, an unknown number of jihadists may have left the United States for other countries; most of those who left were probably Somali and went to Somalia. Other individuals who were suspected of involvement in terrorist activity were arrested for lesser or unrelated crimes and deported when they were found to be in the Untied States illegally.

In addition, some Arab and Muslim immigrants with visa violations were deported. In 2002, the United States began the National Security Entry-Exit Registration System (NSEERS), an attempt to uncover the suspected armies of "sleepers"—terrorist infiltrators— that some believed were in the country. Foreigners who arrived in the United States from certain Arab and Muslim countries were fingerprinted, photographed, and interviewed. Males between the ages of 16 and 45 already in the United States but from the designated countries and without legal permanent resident or refugee status were required to register with U.S. authorities. In the face of widespread complaints about discrimination, the program was scaled back in 2003 and suspended in 2011.

Reportedly, 85,000 men registered between 2002 and 2003. Deportation proceedings were initiated against more than 13,000 of them, and 2,870 were detained for various violations. How many were deported is unknown; proceedings continue in some cases. Only 11 were suspected of terrorist ties, and none were ever charged with terrorist-related crimes.[3]

In addition to the NSEERS program, the Department of Justice established the Foreign Terrorist Tracking Force on October 31, 2001. Its mission was to neutralize "potential terrorist threats by getting violators off the streets by any lawful means possible, as quickly as possible." With the Constitution protecting U.S. citizens, the focus of this effort was on non-citizens, using both criminal and immigration laws. In the first seven weeks of the force's existence, according to Department of Justice figures, 1,182 persons were detained, some of them for long periods. Ultimately, five persons were charged with crimes related to terrorism—three non-citizens plus two U.S. citizens as material witnesses. Of these, James Ujamma and Mahar Hawash were convicted.

Comparison with Europe

Terrorism plots by homegrown jihadists have been uncovered in Canada and Australia, but it is Europe, with its large Muslim population, that has seen the most serious jihadist threat.[4] Authorities there see self-radicalization and recruitment of local residents to jihadist terrorism, or "Islamic terrorism" (the preferred term in Europe), as a major security risk, especially in the United Kingdom, France, Spain, Germany, Belgium, the Netherlands, and, more recently, the Nordic countries.

How do the numbers of individuals involved in jihadist terrorist activities in the United States compare with the numbers in Europe? Differences in definitions, criteria, security policies, and policing practices make it difficult to be sure that one is comparing apples to apples. According to one Dutch official, since 9/11, between 325 and 350 persons have been convicted of offenses related to jihadist terrorism in Europe.[5] Europol, however, gives much higher figures for arrests. On average, European authorities arrest some 200 individuals on terrorism-related charges every year. According to Europol statistics, police in the member states of the European Union arrested 257 "suspects for Islamic terrorism" in 2006, 201 in 2007, 187 in 2008, 110 in 2009, and 179 in 2010, for a total of 934 over the five-year period.[6] France and Spain account for the vast majority of the arrests. Because of different reporting criteria, these figures exclude the United Kingdom.[7] Adding the United Kingdom would increase the total.

This is a much higher number than that given by the Dutch official, although he was referring to convictions, while the Europol numbers are arrests. The difference between these numbers would suggest a much lower success rate in prosecutions, or it may reflect preventive

---

[3] Sam Dolnick, "U.S. Registry Ends, but Not Fallout," *International Herald Tribune*, June 1, 2011.

[4] Most of the al Qaeda–inspired terrorist attacks since 9/11 have occurred in Muslim countries—Morocco, Algeria, Tunisia, Egypt, Jordan, Turkey, Iraq, Yemen, Afghanistan, and Indonesia. No al Qaeda–inspired attacks have occurred in Latin America.

[5] Edwin Bakker, Presentation at the International Security Forum 2011, Zurich, Switzerland, May 31, 2011.

[6] Europol, *TE-SAT 2011: EU Terrorism and Trend Report*, 2011; Eoropol, *Europol Report 2009*, 2010.

[7] According to UK Home Office Statistics, authorities in the United Kingdom made 209 arrests for terrorist actions in 2009 and 125 in 2010, but these include all terrorists, not just those specifically related to al Qaeda or other jihadist groups. The United Kingdom does not publish a breakdown by cause or group. However, 22 percent of those arrested in 2010 were classified as Asian, 34 percent of the arrests resulted in a charge, and 50 percent of the charges were terrorism-related.

strategies aimed at breaking up terrorist cells and possible plots and less concern about eventual prosecutions. Police in European countries are seen to have a freer hand in making arrests, and in some countries, they can hold suspects for longer periods without bringing charges against them. But while police may use information gained through intelligence techniques to prevent terrorist attacks, some European countries have strict rules governing its use in prosecution.

During the same period (2006–2010), 112 persons were arrested for jihadist terrorist activity in the United States, and they experienced a very high conviction rate. According to New York University's Center on Law and Security, which uses a somewhat broader criterion for jihadist cases than that used in this paper, of 308 defendants who were charged with terrorism or related national security crimes since 9/11, 200 cases have been resolved, with convictions obtained in 174 (or 87 percent) of them.[8]

This disparity in numbers between Europe and the United States also may be due to the fact that Europe has a much larger Muslim population. There is no precise figure for the total number of Muslims in the United States, but estimates run between 1.4 million and 3 million—less than 0.5 to 1 percent of the total population. The Muslim population of Europe is estimated to be anywhere between 12 million and 20 million, or 2 to 4 percent of the European Union's total population of about 490 million, with Muslim populations much higher in Western European than in Eastern European countries.

With a Muslim population from four to 14 times that of the United States, depending on which estimate is used, Europe could be expected to have more arrests of jihadists. Assuming something in the middle, say, that Europe's Muslim population is roughly eight or nine times that of the United States, one might expect eight or nine times the number of jihadists. Between 2006 and 2010, 8.3 times more jihadist suspects were arrested in Europe than in the United States—about what might be expected. That would suggest that despite popular perceptions, radicalization and recruitment to terrorism occurs no more frequently in Europe than in the United States. Before accepting this conclusion, however, we would need a more detailed analysis of the reporting criteria.

The real difference is in the quality of activity. While most terrorist plots in the United States have not gone beyond the discussion stage, Europe has suffered some spectacular jihadist terrorist attacks. These include the bombing of Madrid's commuter trains on March 11, 2004, which caused 191 deaths, and the suicide bombings on London's public transport on July 7, 2005, which caused 52 deaths. The failed terrorist attempts and terrorist plots uncovered and foiled by authorities in Europe have also been far more serious than those in the United States.[9]

Profile of the Recruits

Many of the individuals identified as jihadists are merely names on indictments, which provide few biographical details. A full understanding of the process of radicalization and recruitment would require more biographical information on the 176 persons who have been identified.

---

[8] The Center on Law and Security, NYU School of Law, *Terrorist Trial Report Card Update April 2011*, New York: New York University, 2011.

[9] For a recent survey of jihadist radicalization in Europe, see Lorenzo Vidino, *Radicalization, Linkage, and Diversity: Current Trends in Terrorism in Europe*, Santa Monica, Calif.: RAND Corporation, OP-333-OSD, 2011.

They are a diverse lot. The ages of the 31 jihadists named in the 2010 cases range from 19 to 63 years. The average age was 34; the median age, 30. They were a bit older than those named in the cases between 2002 and 2009, whose average age was 31 and whose median age was 27. The overall average age of the entire group was 32, and the median age was 27. Not surprisingly, those joining terrorist groups abroad or plotting to carry out terrorist attacks in the United States tend to be six or seven years younger than those charged with providing material support.

Information on the citizenship of those arrested, indicted, or otherwise identified since 9/11 is incomplete. We do have information for those identified in the 2010 cases: Nine were born in the United States, 14 were naturalized, and two were listed as U.S. citizens, but no information was available on how their citizenship was acquired. One individual was a legal permanent resident, and the citizenship status of the remaining five is not known.

Overall, 76 of the 176 individuals (43 percent) are known to be U.S.-born citizens; at least 49 (27 percent) are naturalized citizens (some became citizens with their parents when they were young); and three are U.S. citizens, but it is not certain whether by birth or by naturalization. In all, 128 (73 percent) of the individuals are U.S. citizens. At least 23 are legal permanent residents. Another 11 are foreign nationals living in the United States, some of whom also may be legal permanent residents. Several are foreign nationals connected with domestic terrorist plots—including the 2007 plot to attack fuel tanks at John F. Kennedy International Airport in New York—who were living abroad. Five entered the country illegally or illegally overstayed their visas. The status of the remaining nine is unknown.

More than half of those identified in the 2010 cases are of Somali origin, while three are Pakistani. The remainder includes immigrants from Egypt, Morocco, and Palestine, as well as the Dominican Republic, Australia, and other non-Muslim countries.

One-quarter of those identified in cases since 9/11 are U.S.-born Americans with non-Muslim surnames. Most of these were converts to Islam. The others have North African, Middle Eastern, South Asian, or Balkan backgrounds. Somalis and Pakistanis predominate, suggesting that immigrant communities with links to war zones are most vulnerable to radicalization and recruitment. (In Europe, Somalis, Algerians, and Pakistanis predominate—all three countries are engaged in major internal conflicts.)

All of those arrested in 2010 except Nadia Rockwell are Muslims. Five of them were converts. Almost all of the jihadists identified to date are Muslims. However, the Liberty City Seven subscribed to eclectic beliefs that most Muslims would regard as heresy, and an opportunity for profit rather than faith motivated a few non-Muslims to propose alliances with terrorists. Some of the Muslims came from families described as secular, but they then adopted a more radical expression of Islam. It is hard to see evidence of extraordinary religious devotion in others. However, a significant percentage—roughly 20 percent—were converts to Islam who displayed the zealotry characteristic of those who embrace new beliefs. A study of 61 homegrown jihadist terrorists by Daveed Gartenstein-Ross and Laura Grossman found that more than 40 percent were converts.[10] Converts are also overrepresented among those arrested for terrorist activity in Europe.

---

[10] Daveed Gartenstein-Ross and Laura Grossman, *Homegrown Terrorists in the U.S. and U.K.: An Empirical Examination of the Radicalization Process,* Washington D.C.: FDD Press, 2009.

Data on education were available for 95 of the individuals named in these cases. Twenty-four had not completed high school, 21 had high school diplomas or their equivalent, 38 were enrolled in or had attended some college, and 12 had graduated from college. Six of the college graduates had gone on to receive postgraduate degrees. The number with a high school education or less coincides roughly with the national average for men 25 and older—47 percent of the jihadists versus 44 percent in the national average—although more jihadists dropped out of high school. More jihadists started college than the national average (many attended local community colleges), but far fewer graduated, since many dropped out in their early twenties to pursue a career in terrorism.

U.S. Terrorists Abroad

Going Abroad to Fight

More than one-quarter of the 176 Americans who have been indicted, arrested, or otherwise identified as jihadist terrorists or their supporters since 9/11, including most of the Somalis, were arrested for recruiting young men to fight abroad or for joining or attempting to join a jihadist front abroad. Since the issue is homegrown terrorism, some may ask why the United States concerns itself with those who leave the country to fight elsewhere. Why, for example, is it the business of the United States if Somalis living in the United States want to return to Somalia to fight Ethiopian invaders, as many did?

Historically, the United States relied on neutrality laws to prevent individuals from recruiting and equipping forces to fight in other countries, although enforcement often has depended on circumstances and political attitudes. In the 19th century, the government sought to prevent American filibusters attempting to mount invasions aimed at toppling governments or seizing territory in Mexico or Central America. During the Mexican Revolution from 1910 to 1920, U.S. authorities selectively arrested Mexicans plotting to overthrow the Mexican government from the U.S. side of the border. The U.S. government, however, did not prevent American volunteers from joining the Canadian or British armies before the United States itself entered World War II.

The current context, however, is completely different and reflects the evolution of American counterterrorism policy. When international terrorism first became a concern of the United States in the early 1970s, the government focused on preventing terrorist incidents. The terrorist groups who hijacked American airliners or kidnapped U.S. diplomats were waging war on foreign governments, not on the United States. The United States had limited opportunities and little inclination to go after them directly. Instead, it focused its diplomatic efforts on ensuring international cooperation in outlawing terrorism, target by target, tactic by tactic.

As terrorist attacks continued, however, the United States sought ways to respond more actively—by providing training and other assistance to cooperative countries; by extending the jurisdiction of U.S. courts so that those who attacked American citizens abroad could, if apprehended, be tried in the United States; by cutting off terrorists' sources of funding; and on limited occasions, by retaliating with military force. In the process, the framework for policy shifted from terrorist incident to terrorist group. This became official in 1996, when terrorist groups were designated as "foreign terrorist organizations." The United States would try to impede everything they did—recruiting, financing, and acquisition of weapons.

With 9/11, combating terrorism became a war. Although the term "War on Terror" caused some confusion, at its core it meant that the United States would employ all the instruments of its power—intelligence, diplomacy, law enforcement, and military force—to destroy al Qaeda and its allies. This included al Qaeda's senior leadership, its various fronts, and groups inspired by its ideology, such as al-Shabaab. American volunteers in these groups would be guilty of providing material support in the form of their services to a foreign terrorist organization. In effect, they would be volunteering to serve on the side of the enemy.

The practical concern is that they could easily end up fighting American forces in Afghanistan or Iraq, which some hoped to do, or that they would provide information to al Qaeda or others that would assist them in planning attacks on American targets, as Bryant Vines was willing to do. The greatest concern was that once having received terrorist training and experience abroad, they would return to carry out terrorist attacks in the United States. This was the case with Faisel Shazad, who tried to set off a bomb in Times Square in 2010.

The Somali Cases

The radicalization and recruitment of Somali-Americans accounts for some of the recent increase in cases. Two of the 15 cases in 2009, involving nine of the 47 individuals named, and eight of the 20 cases in 2010, involving 18 of the 31 new individuals named, were connected to al-Shabaab. In these two years, at least 27 individuals were identified as joining or supporting al-Shabaab's campaign in Somalia. This is hardly a landslide in a Somali-American community estimated to consist of 100,000 to 200,000 people, but it is worth a closer look.

The Somali-American community may be particularly vulnerable to radicalization and recruitment, since Somalis are very poorly prepared immigrants. Coming to the United States as refugees from Somalia's endless conflicts, fewer of them speak English than other recent immigrants. Not easily assimilated, some Somali communities remain socially isolated. Unemployment is especially high. Gangs are a major problem. At the same time, there is great diversity among and within the various Somali communities in the United States. Most of the recruiting has taken place in Minneapolis.

Somalis currently living in the United States look with dismay at the continuing violence perpetuated by Somalia's warring clans and private militias, which they themselves had fled. But it was the 2006 invasion of Somalia, a Muslim country, by Ethiopia, a Christian country and Somalia's historic enemy, that was a catalytic event. The invasion aroused strong sentiments against the United States, especially among some younger Somalis. The United States had backed the invasion as part of an effort to drive out the Islamic Courts Union, elements of which were perceived to be radical supporters of al Qaeda's ideology, but many Somalis saw Ethiopia's occupation of Somalia as a summons to national resistance.

That resistance was spearheaded by al-Shabaab, which almost immediately reached out to the Somalia diaspora for support. For some Somalis who came to the United States as youngsters and are now struggling with their identity as teens and adults, fighting against the Ethiopian occupation was a cause nobler than joining the local street gangs. It was an alluringly dangerous adventure that offered them a chance to demonstrate their manhood and earn their battle scars, and for some, a place in paradise as holy warriors in a heroic struggle. Somalia offered an attractive destination for would-be jihadists, as al-Shabaab welcomed foreign fighters. Furthermore, Somalia's borders are wide open, and neighboring countries are distracted by internal conflicts.

Recruiting in the Somali community began soon after the Ethiopian invasion. Some of the recruiters themselves had participated in earlier rounds of fighting in Somalia and returned to the United States as veterans full of war stories. One of the recruiters promised recruits that jihad would be fun. Recruiting was assisted by Omar Hammami, who, swathed in scarves and bandoliers, became al-Shabaab's leading American voice. In Somalia, he made videos urging others in America to join him. Still, only a trickle of Somali volunteers, perhaps some 20 in all, answered the call and traveled to Somalia to sign up for jihad between 2007 and 2009.

One of those was Shirwa Ahmed, a Somali-born naturalized U.S. citizen who died in a suicide attack in Mogadishu in October 2008, becoming America's first known suicide bomber. An investigation into how Ahmed got to Somalia in the first place led to the discovery that other Somali-Americans had disappeared from the large Somali community in the Minneapolis area. This set off alarms. Al-Shabaab was emerging as the main challenger to the Transitional Government of Somalia, which was backed by the West and now defended by Ethiopian troops. It was also clear that al-Shabaab subscribed to the radical ideology of al Qaeda. Recruiting fighters for Somalia was one thing, but U.S. authorities worried that Americans recruited into al-Shabaab would eventually return to the United States as terrorist operatives.

This concern prompted a nationwide effort in which the FBI and local police departments focused on cities with large Somali-American communities. As part of this effort, the New York Police Department's Strategic Intelligence Unit, which had already been looking at radicalization among young Somalis in New York City, met with local law enforcement officials in Buffalo and Albany, New York; Portland and Lewiston, Maine; and Boston, Massachusetts, to establish working relationships and share information. Meanwhile, FBI officials worked with local police in San Diego, California, and Columbus, Ohio, where there are large populations of Somalis. The National Counterterrorism Center (NCTC) and the Central Intelligence Agency (CIA) also shared essential information. Informed of what was going on in their own communities, alarmed Somali-Americans themselves joined the effort to end the recruiting.

These investigative efforts soon began to produce results. Fourteen individuals, 13 of whom were Somalis, were indicted in 2009 on charges related to recruiting local Somalis and providing support to al-Shabaab. Further indictments and arrests followed in 2010. In August 2010, the U.S. Department of Justice announced four indictments charging 14 persons with providing money, personnel, and services to al-Shabaab. These included 10 men in Minnesota, seven of whom had been identified in the 2009 indictment. These men were charged with attempting to join al-Shabaab or recruiting others to join. Omar Hammami and Jehad Serwan Mostafa, already in Somalia, were charged with being members of al-Shabaab. In a separate indictment, two women in Minnesota were charged with raising money on behalf of al-Shabaab.

In October 2010, federal authorities arrested three more Somali men in San Diego and another in Anaheim, California, for attempting to recruit fighters and for raising funds for al-Shabaab. In a separate case, a Somali resident of Missouri and another from Minnesota were arrested for sending money to al-Shabaab. In November, a Somali woman in San Diego was arrested for attempting to recruit fighters and raise funds for al-Shabaab.

Meanwhile, in June 2010, authorities arrested two men who were not Somalis but who sought to travel to Somalia to join al-Shabaab. Two more men on their way to join al-Shabaab were arrested later in 2010. A young Somali-American in Portland, Oregon, apparently unconnected with the Somali recruiting and fundraising circles elsewhere in the country, was arrested for attempting to detonate a bomb at a Christmas-tree-lighting ceremony in Portland. This is the only case thus far of a Somali-American demonstrating an intention to carry out terrorist attacks in the United States. As the various investigations continue, however, there may be further arrests.

The Somali recruiting cases are the closest thing we have seen to a continuing underground enterprise in the United States. They illustrate the rapid changes that can occur in diaspora communities as a consequence of events abroad. The Somali recruiting investigation is also the first example of a coordinated nationwide domestic intelligence-collection and information-sharing effort aimed at quickly increasing knowledge of a particular diaspora community, alerting its members to recruiting efforts within it, and enlisting their support in discouraging their young men from going to Somalia.

Recruiting in Diaspora Communities Is Not New

In the context of a war on terrorism, the recruiting of Somalis in the United States has aroused understandable concern, but recruiting in diaspora communities is hardly a new phenomenon in America. Much of the terrorist activity in America from the late 1960s to the late 1980s derived from foreign quarrels. Newly arrived Cuban refugees continued a low-level terrorist campaign against Fidel Castro's regime. Inspired by war stories told by their fathers and uncles, young Cuban-Americans carried on the struggle well into the 1970s. In the 1970s and 1980s, young Armenian-Americans were inspired to attack representatives of Turkey's government in an effort to force Turkey to admit its culpability for the 1915 massacre of Armenians. The Provisional Irish Republican Army (IRA) neither trusted nor welcomed American volunteers, but Irish-American supporters provided ample financial support to the IRA cause. This support was outlawed by the United States and eventually reduced.

Puerto Rican separatists continued a decades-long campaign of violence on the U.S. mainland. Croatian separatists in the Croatian community, fighting what they called domination by Southern Slavs, targeted Yugoslav officials in the United States. Radical elements of the Jewish Defense League attacked Soviet and Arab targets.

Many of these earlier terrorist groups focused their violence on the representatives of, or those doing business with, specific foreign countries—Turkey, Yugoslavia, Cuba, various Arab states—rather than the general public. Few sought large-scale casualties, although more people were killed in terrorist attacks in the 1970s than have been killed in the decade following 9/11.

Though by no means comparable to today's terrorists, earlier generations of Americans in far greater numbers, for reasons of ideology, faith, or individual conscience, volunteered to participate in foreign wars, sometimes in defiance of American law. In the late 1940s, hundreds of Americans, many of them veterans of World War II, joined the Machal to fight for Israel's independence. The 1930s saw thousands of Americans joining the International Brigade to fight in Spain's Civil War. In the Spanish case, ideology, not national or religious affinity, motivated the volunteers, but in 1912, hundreds of Greek-Americans left the United States to join the Greek Army in the Balkan wars.

There was in America widespread sympathy and support for these causes at the time, although International Brigade veterans later became targets of suspicion because of their presumed communist sympathies. The point is that distant conflicts have often found recruits and support in American society. Therefore, that al-Shabaab, which was not declared a foreign terrorist organization until 2008, should find a few dozen recruits and fundraisers in the American Somali community is neither unprecedented nor surprising.

Radicalization and Recruitment to Terrorism

Communications and the Importance of the Internet

Many of the jihadists identified in the cases discussed here began their journey toward radicalization on the Internet, where they found resonance and reinforcement for their frustration and anger. (In my view, the biggest danger posed by al Qaeda's ideology is that it will become a conveyer of personal discontents, encouraging violence, legitimizing aggression, and giving it direction.)

Al Qaeda's goal has always been to build an army of believers. Communication, according to Osama bin Laden, is 90 percent of the struggle. Given the operational requirements of clandestinity, which preclude traditional press conferences, face-to-face interviews, and physical broadcasting or printing facilities, and keeping in mind al Qaeda's youthful audience, it is hardly surprising that the Internet has become the primary vehicle for disseminating the organization's propaganda and operational guidance, or that it plays a key role in its overall strategy. According to a Middle Eastern security official, al Qaeda today does 99 percent of its work on the Internet.[11] More than just a communications tool, technology is shaping the nature of the struggle and creating opportunities, as well as dangers, for the terrorist movement.

Forced to operate in a dangerous physical environment since 9/11, al Qaeda has sought cover in cyberspace, reconfiguring its campaign to reflect its new circumstances. Determined to continue the terrorist campaign that is essential to its relevance but compelled to depend more on its affiliates and homegrown terrorists, al Qaeda has expanded its online presence. Whereas only a handful of jihadist websites existed in 2001, there are reportedly thousands today. In their early years, jihadist websites demanded a knowledge of Arabic, but the number of English-language websites reportedly has increased to several hundred, making al Qaeda's message more accessible to the West.[12] Al Qaeda has increased its capacity in other Western languages as well.

The proliferation of websites reflects a deliberate effort by the al Qaeda movement to exploit this new channel of communication, as well as growing interest in the activity of radicalization and recruitment to jihadist terrorism, but it also reflects the growth of cyberspace itself. The increased number of websites devoted to jihadist terrorism is matched by equal increases in the number of websites devoted to astrology, online gambling, or any other topic.

---

[11] M. D. Humaidan, "Scholar Warns Against Al-Qaeda's Recruitment of Youth via Internet," *Arab News,* January 15, 2011, citing a study by Colonel Faiz Al-Shihri.

[12] Gabriel Weinmann, *Terror on the Internet: The New Arena, the New Challenges,* Washington, D.C.: United States Institute for Peace, 2006; Michael Moss and Souad Mekhennet, "An Internet Jihad Aims at U.S. Viewers," *The New York Times,* October 15, 2007.

Communications with potential American recruits have been further facilitated by such native-born Americans as Adam Gadahn, Anwar al-Awlaki, and Omar Hammami, who have become official spokesmen for the al Qaeda core group in Pakistan, al Qaeda in the Arabian Peninsula, and al-Shabaab in Somalia. Although these individuals joined these fronts as volunteers, their prominent role as communicators reflects the strategic importance the movements place on communicating with an American audience.

While Hammami invited Americans to join him in Somalia, the exhortations to violence of American-born radical cleric Anwar al-Awlaki, now living in Yemen, appear to have had some success in persuading individuals to carry out attacks in the United States. Michael Finton and Nidal Hasan, both arrested in 2009, saw al-Awlaki as a spiritual enabler and guide to action. Al-Awlaki also appears to have been a source of inspiration to individuals in at least six of the 20 cases in 2010, including El-Hanafi and Hasanoff, Alessa and Almonte, Samir Khan, Paul Rockwood, Zachery Chesser, and Shaker Masri.

The latest component in al Qaeda's propaganda campaign is *Inspire*, an online magazine published under the auspices of al Qaeda in the Arabian Peninsula. *Inspire* promotes individual, violent jihad. It reinforces al Qaeda's narrative, profiles jihadists, and offers suggestions for simple attacks and practical instructions for building improvised weapons and bombs. The producers of *Inspire* probably also see the publication as part of the continuing campaign of terror, hoping that by describing methods of attack, they can spread fear and rattle the nerves of those charged with security, who must now answer questions about how they plan to prevent such attacks.

Inspire is the creation of Samir Khan, a naturalized U.S. citizen who moved to the United States from Saudi Arabia with his parents when he was seven years old. He began his own journey to violent jihad when he was 15. He reportedly left the United States in late 2009, resurfacing in Yemen in 2010.

Inspire targets an audience of English-speaking young men in their twenties. Khan himself is 24. While the publication repeats al Qaeda's ideology of global struggle and includes supporting quotes from the Koran, the emphasis is on action, not theology. Some of the articles in *Inspire* remind one of those in earlier men's adventure magazines such as *Argosy* and *Saga*, while the how-to pieces recall Carlos Marighella's *Minimanual of the Urban Guerrilla* and *The Anarchist's Cookbook*. Readers of these earlier manuals pored over them as if they contained pornography. This was hard-core stuff, not mind-numbing ideological treatises but instructions on how to carry out a kidnapping or build a bomb. One issue of *Inspire* provided instructions on how to disassemble and clean a Kalashnikov rifle, the weapon of choice in Afghanistan. Probably not many of *Inspire*'s readers in America or England own Kalashnikovs, but the article was intended to make the domestic reader feel connected with real-world fighters.

In marketing terms, there are now more retail outlets, more salesmen who know the territory and are able to speak in their constituents' own language, and more content that is appealing to an audience of angry young men looking for meaning, hankering for status, and seeking adventure.

The communications campaign is not the creation of an al Qaeda media mogul. It is a distributed effort beginning at the top with al Qaeda's leaders, who still manage to deliver video and audio commentary to an underground contingent of techies, who, in turn, ensure sophisticated presentation and distribution on the Internet, where the messages are received, further embellished, and widely discussed. But the online jihad is no longer a matter of waiting for word from the top. Production has exploited new web platforms that allow users to also become producers of material. Although websites can still be distinguished hierarchically between official communications and more democratic discourse, the online jihad has become a parallel universe to the physical world of bombs and burnt flesh.

Previously, al Qaeda's leaders saw the Internet as a vehicle to awaken and energize followers to take up arms in the real world, but online contributions to the jihadist cause are now recognized by al Qaeda as being just as important as physical action. By valuing these contributions, Qaeda now accepts what it previously would have deemed as inadequate zeal. It is, in effect, lowering the bar of physical commitment in order not to alienate its online army, but doing so also points to weaknesses in al Qaeda's Internet strategy. Why is it not working?

The Internet serves as a source of inspiration, but it may also become a substitute for action, allowing would-be terrorists to safely engage in vicarious terrorism while avoiding the risks of real action, in which case al Qaeda and its allies have created a virtual army that thus far has remained virtual. (It is fascinating to note that one of the many explanations for America's falling violent crime rate is the advent of the Internet and videogames, which provide risk-free thrills and keep young men off the streets and away from real crime.) Reaching does not mean radicalizing, and radicalizing does not mean recruitment to violent jihad. The Internet has facilitated access to many more recruits than al Qaeda could reach personally, but it is low-yield mining. The ranks of online jihadists, no doubt swollen by masquerading intelligence operatives pretending to be jihadists, include the merely curious as well as those who may be attracted by the ideology or the glamour. Talking about jihad, boasting of what one will do, and offering diabolical schemes egging each other on is usually as far as it goes. It may provide psychological satisfaction to its authors and win accolades from other pretend warriors, but it is primarily an outlet for verbal expression, not an anteroom to violence.

Although the Internet clearly contributes to radicalization, and possibly to recruitment to jihadist terrorism, it has not yet produced the army of action-oriented acolytes sought by al Qaeda's leaders. In the 1970s and 1980s, before the Internet became widely used, ethnic-based terrorist groups in the United States were comparatively better organized, and collectively they were able to recruit numbers equal to—certainly not significantly smaller than—today's jihadist collective. They also were able to sustain their terrorist campaigns over a period of years, something America's jihadist terrorists thus far have been unable to do.

Some have suggested that al Qaeda is employing a strategy of "gamification," providing forums where followers share violent fantasies as a means of encouraging them toward real violence. However, it is not clear that this is, in fact, al Qaeda's strategy—sometimes too-clever analysts get ahead of their subjects. Nor do we know if online blooding will lead to real-life blood.

It is also possible, however, that in what promises to be a long struggle, we are only on the leading edge of a wave of homegrown terrorism, in which online jihadists, emboldened by the actions of others or propelled by events and tutored by Internet manuals, will push back from their computer screens to launch more and more-significant attacks.

The Path to Terrorism

Radicalization and recruitment to jihadist terrorism appears to be very much an individualistic process that combines external factors and personal circumstances. Of those who adopt radical views, only a few go further toward terrorist violence.

Young men are attracted to jihadist terrorism for a variety of reasons. They may be disillusioned with their current circumstances. They may be propelled by religious faith, seeing fighting as their duty, although we do not know whether faith pushes people toward violence or justifies extant aggression. With the exception of a few con men and mercenaries, all of the 176 recruits since 9/11 have been Muslims, but fervent faith itself does not explain becoming a jihadist terrorist. Volunteer jihadists may see terrorism as an opportunity to demonstrate their virility as warriors. Events may trigger radicalization. Recruits may seek revenge for perceived injustices inflicted on themselves or their communities. They may want adventure and glory. They may be swept along by friends or by forceful personalities who become their guides and give them direction. Much is happenstance, depending on whom the recruits encounter. Dissatisfied with life, they may seek paradise. Al Qaeda appeals to all of these motives.

Research has identified phases or stages in the process of radicalization and recruitment to jihadist terrorism, beginning with a personal search that leads to the adoption of a new worldview—the embrace of new beliefs—followed by the hardening of this view, leading to the violent path offered by al Qaeda and ultimately a commitment to action. There is, however, more than a single path, and the journey is not an arc, which looking only at those arrested might suggest. Individuals may move through the anteroom of radicalization in a straight line toward terrorism or meander about its periphery for months, even years, while recalibrating their commitment.

Some individuals may drop out of the movement because they disapprove of terrorism or personally have no desire to kill. They may not be certain about their newfound beliefs. They may shy from the danger of death or become convinced by the continuing public exposure of terrorist plots that they too will be arrested and imprisoned—an inglorious fate. (Others, knowing that they were being watched by authorities, have persisted in their preparations, carelessly disregarding the likelihood of capture.) Just as peer pressure may drag some toward terrorism, intervention by family or friends may dissuade others from a destructive and self-destructive path. In some cases, other opportunities may come along. Those heading toward radicalization may fall in love and get married. Since dropouts do not announce themselves to authorities, there is no way of knowing how many there have been, but it is possible that at any moment, there is a floating population of might-become terrorists mixed with a much smaller number of would-be terrorists.

This poses problems for the authorities, who are confronted with monitoring many individuals, knowing that only a fraction may do something that merits arrest. It means initiating thousands of investigations, most of which will produce no result.

There is further risk in that once an individual rises to the level of official attention, he cannot be easily ignored, even if he is judged at the time to pose little risk. If, much later, that same individual participates in a terrorist attack and it is discovered that he was looked at and dismissed as a danger, the organization that ignored him will pay a political price.

One way of finding out who might be dangerous is to probe intentions with sting operations, which lubricate the suspect's decisionmaking. Instead of monitoring a subject for months, perhaps years, the undercover law enforcement organization offers him the means to take action and watches to see if he goes for it. We do not know how many suspects back out once the talk turns serious. We know only about those who go all the way to joining a terrorist group or plotting to carry out a terrorist attack.

A Closer Look at the Terrorist Plots

Six of the 20 cases in 2010 involved attempts or intentions to carry out terrorist attacks in the United States. (There were eight such plots in 2009.) Faisal Shahzad constructed an incendiary device that he hoped to ignite in New York's Times Square. If that had worked, Shahzad planned to follow up with further attacks on other targets. Paul Rockwood discussed plans to kill 15 individuals who, in his view, had offended Islam, and he researched how to build explosive devices. Authorities did not reveal his list of targets. Farooque Ahmed intended to attack Washington, D.C., Metro stations, and he selected specific stations at which he told undercover FBI agents bombs should be placed. His intention was to kill as many military personnel as possible. Mohamed Osman Mohamud wanted to detonate a car bomb at a Christmas-tree-lighting ceremony in Portland, Oregon, in order to cause mass casualties. Testing his intentions, undercover FBI agents provided him with a fake bomb, which he tried to detonate. Antonio Martinez intended to blow up the Armed Forces Career Center in Catonsville, Maryland. He, too, was provided with a fake bomb by FBI agents who had been in contact with him for two months. Finally, Raja Lahrasib Khan reportedly made vague references to attacking an unspecified stadium, but his operational plan reportedly consisted of uttering the words, "Boom, boom, boom, boom." Three of these six cases involved FBI stings.

Since 9/11, there have been 32 homegrown jihadist plots to carry out attacks in the United States. Most of these plots never got beyond the discussion stage, although a few got as far as reconnaissance before being interrupted by authorities. In only 10 cases had the plotters developed an operational plan that identified a specific place to attack, decided upon or acquired the weapons to be used, and laid out the sequence of what they intended to do. Six of these 10 cases involved FBI stings. This suggests that while America's jihadist terrorists have lethal intentions, they have trouble getting their act together on their own. Three of the 32 cases of plots to carry out terrorist attacks in the United States involved six or more persons, but 22 (69 percent) of them involved only a single individual.

However, considering these individuals to be loners is misleading. Closer examination shows that at least seven of the individuals in these cases were working for al Qaeda at the time of their arrest, and one was supported by the Pakistan Taliban. Another, Carlos Bledsoe, had spent time in Yemen and later claimed to be an al Qaeda operative, but he may not have been one. Eight of the individuals were working with FBI informants or undercover agents whom they believed to be part of al Qaeda. They had connected with a group, but it was not the one they intended to connect with. In fact, not counting Bledsoe, only two could be called true locally created loners: Derrick Shareef and Nidal Hasan. Lone terrorists who radicalize and plot terrorist attacks on their own, albeit with Internet encouragement, are rare. Terrorist plotting is a social activity in which sharing violent fantasies is itself a source of psychological pleasure. Lone terrorists are very rare, but they are also harder to identify.

In three of the terrorist plots, specific targets were not identified. In seven cases where targets were discussed, and the only two in which the attackers managed to kill anyone, military facilities—the Marine Corps base at Quantico, Virginia; National Guard armories; armed forces recruiting centers; soldiers at Fort Dix and Fort Hood—were the targets. In the remaining 23 cases, numerous targets were identified.

Attacks in easily accessible places of public assembly (subway stations, shopping malls, Times Square, and central Portland) predominated. Four cases mentioned possible attacks on infrastructure—electrical substations, the Brooklyn Bridge, the Alaska Pipeline, and fuel tanks at JFK Airport. Los Angeles International Airport was also mentioned as a possible target in one case. Three cases involved intended attacks on prominent office buildings in Chicago, Washington, D.C., and Dallas; two cases involved intended attacks on federal buildings in Florida and Illinois. A synagogue in New York, unspecified synagogues in Florida and California, and the Israeli consulate were other possible targets mentioned in the plots. Assassinations made up the remaining three intended attacks. The targets were the president of the United States, Pakistani diplomats, and a list of persons who had offended Islam.

While targets were discussed in most of the terrorist plots, they were usually generic or theoretical. For example, terrorists referred to blowing up shopping malls or attacking synagogues but did not specify any in particular, or they identified large systems or installations but not specific points of attack. Bryant Vinas offered the Taliban information about the Long Island Rail Road. Michael Reynolds discussed the Alaska Pipeline. Plotters in New Jersey wanted to attack soldiers at Fort Dix.

Only 13 targets were specifically identified. In 10 of these cases, the terrorists developed an operational plan, but only three of the attacks were carried out: Bledsoe's attack on the Army Recruiting Center in Little Rock, Arkansas; Nidal Hasan's attack at Fort Hood, Texas; and Faisal Shahzad's failed attempt at Times Square. The remaining cases involved federal undercover agents. And the questions that agents ask—What do you intend to attack? How will you do it?—oblige the plotters to think more concretely about whether they want to go ahead and do something, what specifically they want to do, and how they intend to do it. This interaction tests the seriousness of their intentions and also produces the specificity that impresses a court, but it also introduces the risk that an agent will subtly begin to shape the plot. That does not diminish the demonstration of terrorist intentions when individuals press the button to detonate what they believe to be real bombs, but each case merits close scrutiny.

Bombs were the weapon of choice in most of the plots, although none of the plotters successfully built an explosive device. Faisal Shahzad built an incendiary device that did not work. Najibullah Zazi acquired the ingredients to make an explosive device and apparently had the knowledge to assemble one, but his need for additional technical guidance from his contact in Pakistan alerted U.S. authorities to his scheme. Paul Rockwood researched how to build bombs. Ronald Grecula offered to make a bomb for undercover law enforcement agents whom he believed to be al Qaeda operatives. In five of the cases, would-be terrorists were equipped with fake bombs by undercover FBI agents.

Four cases involved firearms; in one of them, the use of bombs and guns was anticipated. The only cases that succeeded in causing casualties were the two involving guns—Carlos Bledsoe's attack on the Army Recruiting office in Little Rock and Nidal Hasan's deadly attack at Fort Hood. In 12 cases, the actual method of attack was not specified.

Of the 32 cases of plots to carry out attacks in the United States, six involved actual connections (beyond the Internet) with terrorist groups abroad. José Padilla and Iyman Faris had direct connections with al Qaeda and could be called al Qaeda operatives, and Nuradin Abdi was arrested in 2004 as an accomplice of Faris. Uzair Paracha was enlisted to get an al Qaeda operative into the country. Carlos Bledsoe spent time in Yemen and months after his arrest claimed to be connected with al Qaeda, although many analysts dismiss this claim as a boast. Bryant Vinas collaborated with al Qaeda in Pakistan, where he was arrested and extradited to the United States. Najibullah Zazi received training at a terrorist camp in Pakistan and was in contact with persons there from whom he sought additional technical instructions.

Faisal Shahzad had received training and financing from Pakistan's Taliban. Jihadist organizations can exploit those who reach them, sending such recruits back to reconnoiter targets and carry out attacks, but apart from the Internet, these organizations apparently have very limited capacity to connect with potential recruits in the United States. This again underscores the importance of the Internet as a means of radicalizing and inspiring (more than "recruiting" in the traditional sense) individuals to carry out terrorist operations. But it also illustrates the need for terrorists to be physically connected in order to gain competence.

Of the entire body of 82 cases, four in addition to those mentioned above involve persons who had received some terrorist training abroad. Twenty-one cases involve Americans leaving or planning to leave the United States to join terrorist groups abroad.

It is difficult to say how many of the terrorist plots would have been successfully carried out had the authorities not intervened. Certainly not all, but perhaps a few would have. All of the plots were meant to kill, but the psychological effect of simply more blood on the ground in a nation already on edge would have been significant. Judging by the reactions to Hasan's attack at Fort Hood and the near misses, successful terrorist attacks would have created political crises, demands for new intelligence arrangements, further costly security measures, and increased hostility toward the Muslim community.

With the exception of the Somali cases, there is very little evidence of connectivity among the recent cases. And again with the Somali exception, almost none of the individuals arrested for supporting jihadist terrorist groups or planning terrorist attacks in the United States had direct contacts with any of the others in the United States. These are primarily one-off responses, unconnected tiny conspiracies or, more often, individuals pursuing their own personal jihads. There seems to be no clandestine underground.

Stray Dogs, Not Lone Wolves

U.S. law enforcement agencies and the news media often employ the term "lone wolf" to refer to self-recruited individuals engaged in terrorist activity.[13] The dictionary defines *lone wolf* as one who goes without the company or assistance of others, but the term has a much richer connotation. In the animal world, a lone wolf leaves the pack to hunt alone. Often stronger and more aggressive than the other wolves, lone wolves are considered more dangerous predators. In literature, "lone wolf" often describes a renegade hero operating outside the law, doing whatever is necessary to get the job done. This is not an accurate description of America's contemporary jihadist terrorists. The term carries the connotation of determination, cunning, strength—a ferocious adversary.

In the 1970s, Italian police used a less flattering term to describe those engaged in violence outside the orbit of the Red Brigades—they were "stray dogs." And indeed, the jihadists' behavior seems to more closely resemble that of stray dogs, who may be found alone or in packs, estranged from but dependent on society, streetwise but lacking social skills, barking defiantly, and potentially dangerous but at the same time, suspicious, fearful, skittish. On their own, few of America's jihadists move in a straight line toward action. They wander about in

---

[13] A "lone wolf" provision, which allows the FBI to surveil individuals who have no nexus to a foreign power or entity, was actually put into law in 2004.

the shade of the jihadist ideology, sniffing at the edges of violence before making a move. Most are arrested before they get that far.

Suicide Attacks Are Rarely Contemplated by American Recruits

Months before 9/11, six young Yemeni-Americans from Lackawanna, New York, traveled to an al Qaeda training camp in Afghanistan. Prior to their return, they were interviewed by Osama bin Laden himself, who asked them how many Americans they thought were ready to become martyrs. They answered that Americans really weren't into suicide attacks. Bin Laden expressed his disappointment.

At least seven Somali-Americans recruited in the United States were reportedly killed while fighting for al-Shabaab in Somalia, but insofar as is known, only one, Shirwa Ahmed, died in a suicide attack.

Since authorities interrupted most of the post-9/11 terrorist plots in the United States long before the plots matured, it is not possible to determine whether the plotters envisioned their attacks to be suicidal. Only two of the cases in which the perpetrators had an operational plan can be described as suicidal: Najibullah Zazi planned to carry out suicide attacks on New York's subways, and in opening fire at Fort Hood, Nidal Hasan had to assume that he would be shot. In the other eight cases, the perpetrators tried or planned to get away.

As noted above, Faisal Shahzad intended to escape and to follow up the Times Square bombing with further attacks. Carlos Bledsoe also planned to escape, as did the would-be terrorists in the other six cases. But every one of these six plots, in its final stages, involved FBI participation. These were stings, set up to demonstrate the subjects' willingness to kill, not test their willingness to die. Pressed to commit suicide, some might have backed out. For operational safety reasons, FBI facilitators also may have shied away from sting operations that put suspects in the position where they thought they would be conducting a suicide attack. A sting that put the subject in a vehicle with a bomb, even a fake bomb, or put him in an explosives vest at the attack venue could cause panic and potential danger to bystanders, who would not know the device was fake. Even if there were no casualties, the reaction of the public to being exposed to such danger would be negative. Scenarios involving detonation at a distance were undoubtedly safer.

Nevertheless, while not excluding the possibility of suicide attacks in the future, it appears that, unlike the jihadists who launched attacks elsewhere in the world, including the 2005 bombing in United Kingdom and, most recently, Sweden, America's homegrown jihadists are simply not contemplating suicide. This does not mean that they are not still lethal; some of the deadliest terrorist attacks, including the 2004 train bombings in Madrid, which killed 191, and the 2006 train bombings in Mumbai, which killed 209, were not suicide attacks.

Does the absence of suicide attacks suggest a low level of commitment that accompanies what is clearly a low level of capability? Al Qaeda itself may believe so, as evidenced by its recent exhortations to homegrown terrorists urging them to carry out low-level attacks.

Assessing the Threat

Slouching Toward Action

Thus far, America has not provided fertile soil for recruiting jihadist terrorists. The turnout has been meager. In addition, most of the 32 plots to carry out terrorist attacks in the United States never got beyond the discussion stage, and most of those that did were stings in which the FBI provided fake bombs. On their own, only two individuals actually attempted to build devices. One was arrested while doing so, and the other's device failed. The rest of the would-be terrorists only talked about bombs.

The two fatal attacks killed a total of 14 people, while 73 people have been killed in hate crimes in the United States since 2001, to say nothing of the sadly not uncommon cases of mentally disturbed shooters gunning down people in murderous rampages and, of course, America's annual homicide rate of between 15,000 and 20,000 murders a year, all of which suggest that killing is not very hard.

These statistics indicate not merely a fortunate lack of competence but also a certain half-heartedness on the part of American jihadists. Those arrested in stings were demonstrably willing to kill if someone handed them the means, but others made little effort to build bombs or acquire guns, which are readily available in the United States. They also suggest that the stings themselves acted as a "psychological accelerant" for those contemplating—and ultimately willing to carry out—terrorist attacks; access to the means provided by undercover agents propelled them to a decision point at which they could either demonstrate their intentions or back out. We do not know how many of the would-be terrorists backed out of such sting operations. Those included in this paper appeared ready to kill. Nonetheless, while prosecutions based on sting operations that prove intentions are superior to prosecutions based solely on the testimony of confidential informants, there is still some reluctance to prosecute on the basis of intentions.

Attitudes of the American Muslim Community

Community attitudes are an important factor in radicalization, but their effects are unequal. Community support facilitates radicalization and permits recruitment, and it allows terrorist violence to persist, while community disapproval may limit radicalization and recruitment to only those who seek to defy the community anyway.

Generally, radicalization and recruitment to jihadist terrorism in America is seen as a law enforcement problem, not a social problem. In the United States, to hold radical views is not considered to be a crime. The Constitution provides strong protection of individual beliefs and free speech. Only when these turn to criminal incitement and violent action or manifest intent to engage in violence is there cause for legal intervention; this is why analysts favor the phrase "radicalization *and* recruitment to terrorist violence." It is the second step that makes the first step a matter of concern.

Nonetheless, some in the United States have voiced concerns about the role of the Muslim community. Some assert that American Muslims are insufficiently patriotic, and they offer anecdotal evidence that Muslims are not cooperating with the authorities in dealing with homegrown terrorism. Some fear that American Muslims will not only resist assimilation of American values but will attempt to gradually impose their beliefs on others through "creeping Sharia." Mirroring al Qaeda's ideology, a few go further and see the religion of Islam itself as aggressive and warn of inevitable religious war, which some seek to provoke, while a handful see Muslim conspiracies in the White House.

The meager turnout of jihadist terrorists suggests that al Qaeda's ideology has little resonance in America's Muslim community. Public opinion surveys show that a vast majority of American Muslims have an unfavorable view of al Qaeda and that just about as many Muslims in America as non-Muslims worry about Islamic extremism.[14] But there are modest traces of support, particularly among those under 30 years of age, although openly declaring favorable opinions of al Qaeda to an American pollster after 9/11 would seem to be more an act of youthful defiance than an indication of future terrorist action. Still, there are hot spots where radical Islam and violent rhetoric are the currency of discourse. These may be located geographically or they may exist only in cyberspace, where individuals scattered among the Muslim population reinforce each other's hostilities online.

The people most likely to observe signs of radicalization tending toward recruitment are family members and close friends of potential recruits, the people who are also best positioned to intervene. Such interventions, when they occur, remain largely invisible to the outside. No one is likely to report that a friend or relative almost became a terrorist.

Failure to dissuade someone from pursuing a course of destruction requires informing the authorities. Again, this is not likely to take the form of public denunciation, but there is anecdotal evidence that it occurs. It is estimated that between one-third and one-half of the known cases began with a tip from within the Muslim community.[15]

There is also anecdotal evidence of instances of non-cooperation, which surely must occur. Much depends on how one defines cooperation. Public denunciations of terrorism in order to demonstrate cooperation may reassure non-Muslims, but they are probably the least effective mode of cooperation in dealing with radicalization.

Muslim Americans understandably resent close scrutiny by authorities, arguing that their religion or ethnicity ought not to make them targets of intelligence or greater scrutiny for security. While discrimination is contrary to American values and law, the social geography of intelligence collection is dictated by the nature of the threat. When the threat of terrorism came from Ku Klux Klan members and other racists responsible for bombing black churches and killing civil rights workers, intelligence efforts focused on white Southerners. When anti-Castro Cubans carried on a bombing campaign in Florida, intelligence efforts focused on the Cuban community. The same was true when the authorities were dealing with Puerto Rican, Armenian, and Jewish terrorists. If the country were threatened by Viking terrorism today,

---

14 Pew Research Center, *Muslim Americans: Middle Class and Mostly Mainstream*, Washington, D.C., May 22, 2007.

15 "Fact Checking the Sunday Shows—March 6, 2011," MediaMatters Action Network, March 7, 2011.

intelligence would have a different focus. Muslim Americans must accept that while religion alone does not make the community a target of the state, neither does it provide immunity from legitimate intelligence and law enforcement investigations within the community.

Potential Future Threats Drive Concerns

Despite the lack of achievement by America's homegrown terrorists thus far, U.S. officials worry about the evolving homegrown terrorist threat. Testifying before the House Homeland Security Committee on February 9, 2011, Homeland Security Secretary Janet Napolitano warned that "the terrorist threat to the homeland is, in many ways, at its most heightened state since 9/11."[16] Michael Leiter, the former director of the NCTC, agreed that homegrown violent extremists continue to pose an elevated threat to the homeland.[17]

These assessments reflect a number of specific concerns. They include al Qaeda's increasing emphasis on homegrown plotting as a way to attack the United States, the organization's growing communications effort aimed at inspiring do-it-yourself terrorists, and the "development of a U.S.-specific narrative that motivates individuals to violence."[18] These concerns are a measure of al Qaeda's investment.

Equally worrisome is the growing role played by al Qaeda affiliate, al Qaeda in the Arabian Peninsula—more specifically, the important inspirational role played by U.S.-born Anwar al-Awlaki and potentially by the group's new online magazine *Inspire*.

U.S. analysts also have worried that the insurgency in Iraq would produce a cadre of experienced terrorist bomb builders and operatives who would then carry their skills with them to launch attacks outside of Iraq. Some terrorist tradecraft has been exported from Iraq to the ongoing conflicts in Afghanistan and Pakistan, but thus far, no Iraqi terrorist diaspora has emerged in Europe or the United States. Nevertheless, it is something that could happen, and U.S. authorities are closely monitoring arriving Iraqi immigrants.

Other terrorist groups, such as Lashkar-e-Toiba and Tehrik-e-Taliban Pakistan, appear to have incorporated al Qaeda's strategy of global terrorism. Tehrik-e-Taliban Pakistan provided instruction and financing for Faisal Shahzad's attempted bombing in Times Square. Somalia's al-Shabaab has sought American recruits but has not supported attacks in the United States, and its recent reported threat to attack the United States is extremely vague. However, U.S. authorities worry that al-Shabaab veterans may in the future return to the United States to carry out attacks.

A more sensitive and less discussed issue is the existence in America of isolated Salafi communities, primarily consisting of recent immigrants. The Salafis are strict Muslim literalists who resist what they see as corruption by American culture, and they will not easily assimi-

---

[16] Testimony of Secretary Janet Napolitano before the U.S. House of Representatives Committee on Homeland Security, "Understanding the Homeland Threat Landscape—Considerations for the 112th Congress," Washington, D.C., February 9, 2011.

[17] Testimony of Michael E. Leiter, Director, National Counterterrorism Center, before the U.S. House of Representatives Committee on Homeland Security, Washington, D.C., February 9, 2011.

[18] James R. Clapper, Statement for the Record on the Worldwide Threat Assessment of the U.S. Intelligence Community for the House Permanent Select Committee on Intelligence, Office of the Director of National Intelligence, February 10, 2011.

late into American society. They are not terrorists—in fact, they condemn al Qaeda's jihadist beliefs as contrary to the Koran—but some subscribe to the worldview of an inevitable clash between Islam and America in which violence is a real possibility.

Salafi America is not a terrorist problem; it remains a social issue. The United States has a great capacity for tolerating self-isolating religious communities, permitting them to exercise their own beliefs as long as these do not violate the law of the land, but on occasion, encounters with some of these communities have turned violent.

Contributing to the continuing alarm about the threat posed by homegrown terrorists is the remarkable string of intelligence successes and good luck that have prevented another significant jihadist terrorist attack on U.S. soil since 9/11, aside from Nidal Hasan's and Carlos Bledsoe's.

Not since the late 1960s has the United States experienced an almost 10-year run without a major terrorist attack on an American target abroad or in the United States. President George W. Bush regarded preventing another terrorist attack on U.S. soil after 9/11 as his "most meaningful accomplishment as president."[19] The prospect of a successful terrorist attack must haunt the current U.S. administration, especially in the partisan environment of contemporary American politics.

As we have seen in the 1995 terrorist bombing in Oklahoma City and the 2011 events in Norway, it requires only one determined, reasonably competent terrorist plotter to hold together a tiny conspiracy or possibly to single-handedly create a terrorist disaster, not one on the scale of 9/11 but one that could cause scores, even hundreds, of casualties. Faisal Shahzad's infernal machine, had it worked, would not have caused hundreds or even thousands of casualties, which has now become the established lore, but given America's unrealistic zero tolerance for risk, a hyperactive news media, and politicians primed to point fingers, even a small-scale incident could easily provoke national overreaction.

An Appreciation of the Current Situation

The numbers speak for themselves. America is not immune to radicalization and recruitment to al Qaeda–inspired ideology and terrorist violence on its behalf, but the turnout is tiny. There are no secret armies of sleepers, no terrorist groups comparable to those of the 1960s and 1970s, no sustained bombing campaigns.

The few terrorists, would-be terrorists, and active supporters of terrorism are for the most part individuals or tiny conspiracies who connected or tried to connect with terrorist groups abroad or believed they had done so while communicating with government agents. Their radicalization and recruitment to terrorism, in person or on the Internet, was not a community phenomenon; it was an individual decision, sometimes unknown to their own families, often in defiance of family members.

The Internet facilitates connecting with jihadist ideologies, but thus far it has not enabled jihadist communicators to mobilize an army. Jihadist sites on the Internet remain an arena for chest-thumping and fantasies of violence, but they may also divert online jihadists from the real thing. Osama bin Laden's death produced plenty of bellicose rhetoric but no explosion of action.

---

[19] George W. Bush, *Decision Points*, New York: Crown Publishers, 2010, p. 181.

Qualitatively, America's jihadist terrorists have not shown great determination or much competence. When provided with bombs, they were willing to act, but only two actually tried to build devices on their own, and only one of these actually built one, which failed to function. In a country where guns are readily available, only two terrorists—and the only two to succeed—took up arms.

America still works. Despite concerns expressed by some, the vast majority of America's Muslim immigrants have assimilated into American society, where for the most part they are doing well. Overwhelmingly, they reject jihadist ideology. Yet there are local diaspora communities struggling with assimilation and closely connected with conflict zones that are vulnerable to recruitment. Policing efforts aimed at enlisting community cooperation and intelligence efforts aimed at preventing and deterring terrorist activity that would endanger society and the Muslim communities themselves will continue.

Despite the growing bibliography devoted to the subject, understanding radicalization and recruitment to jihadist terrorism is still a work in progress. Many questions remain about the role of conversions (including internal conversion to extremist beliefs within the Muslim religion), the important differences between the Somali recruits and others attracted to jihadist terrorism, the role of the Internet, and trends in recruiting and in the composition of recruits over time. These will have relevance to policy discussions, radicalization and de-radicalization efforts, and American attitudes about the issue.

Chronology of the Cases

2002

- **José Padilla.** *José Padilla* (32), a native U.S. citizen, convert to Islam, and al Qaeda operative, was arrested upon his return from the Middle East to the United States. Although there is no question of his al Qaeda connection, his mission remains unclear. He was convicted for providing material support to al Qaeda and sentenced in 2008. A co-defendant, *Kifah Wael Jayyousi* (40), a naturalized U.S. citizen from Jordan, was also convicted.

- **The Lackawanna Six.** Six Yemeni-Americans—*Sahim Alwar* (26), *Yahya Goba* (25), *Yasein Taher* (24), *Faysal Galab* (25), *Shafal Mosed* (23), all born in the United States, and *Muktar al-Bakri* (21), a naturalized citizen—were arrested for training at an al Qaeda camp in Afghanistan.

- **The Portland Seven.** Seven individuals—*Patrice Lumumba Ford* (31), *Jeffrey Leon Battle* (31), *October Martinique Laris* (25), *Muhammad Ibrahim Bilal* (22), *Ahmed Ibrahim Bilal* (24), all native U.S. citizens; *Habis Abdulla al Saoub* (37), a U.S. permanent resident from Jordan; and *Maher Hawash* (38), a naturalized U.S. citizen from Jordan—were arrested for attempting to join al Qaeda and the Taliban.

- **Earnest James Ujaama.** *Earnest James Ujaama* (36), a native U.S. citizen, was arrested for providing support to the Taliban.

- **Imran Mandhai.** *Imran Mandhai* (20), a U.S. permanent resident from Pakistan, told an FBI informant that he wanted to wage war against the United States. He planned to assemble an al Qaeda cell and attack various targets in Florida, including electrical substations, Jewish businesses, a National Guard armory, and also, improbably, Mount Rushmore. Under surveillance for a long time, Mandhai was arrested and subsequently convicted of conspiracy to destroy property.

- **Anwar al-Awlaki.** *Anwar al-Awlaki* (31), a U.S. citizen born in New Mexico, studied engineering in college and motivation in graduate school, then became an increasingly radical imam. After being questioned by the FBI several times, he left the United States in 2002 and went to Yemen, where he is now a leading spokesperson for al Qaeda.

2003

- **Adnan Gulshair el Shukrijumah.** A provisional arrest warrant was issued for *Adnan Gulshair el Shukrijumah* (27), a Saudi national and legal permanent resident, who grew up and worked in the United States. Shukrijumah was suspected of involvement in a number of terrorist plots. In 2010, he was indicted for his involvement in the 2009 Zazi plot to blow up New York subways.

- **Iyman Faris.** *Iyman Faris* (34), a naturalized U.S. citizen from Pakistan, was arrested for reconnoitering the Brooklyn Bridge for a possible al Qaeda attack.

- **The Northern Virginia Cluster.** Eleven men were arrested in June 2003 for training at a jihadist training camp abroad, intending to join Lashkar-e-Toiba, and planning terrorist attacks: *Caliph Basha Ibn Abdur Raheem* (28), a native U.S. citizen; *Sabri Benkhala* (27), a native U.S. citizen; *Randoll Todd Royer* (39), a native U.S. citizen; *Ibrahim al-Hamdi* (25), a Yemeni national; *Khwaja Mahmood Hasan* (27), a naturalized U.S. citizen from Pakistan; *Muhammed Aatique* (30), a legal permanent resident from Pakistan; *Donald T. Surratt* (30), a native U.S. citizen; *Masoud Ahmad Khan* (33), a naturalized U.S. citizen from Pakistan; *Seifullah Chapman* (31), a native U.S. citizen; *Hammad Abdur-Raheem* (34), a U.S.-born citizen and Army veteran of the first Gulf War; and *Yong Ki Kwon* (27), a naturalized U.S. citizen from Korea. Two other individuals were also arrested in connection with the group: *Ali al-Timimi* (40), a U.S.-born citizen, and *Ali Asad Chandia* (26), a citizen of Pakistan. Six of the accused pleaded guilty, and another three were convicted. Benkhala was acquitted but was later charged and convicted of making false statements to the FBI. Al-Timimi was convicted in 2005. The case against Caliph Basha Ibn Abdur Raheem was dismissed.

- **Uzair Paracha.** *Uzair Paracha* (23), a legal permanent resident from Pakistan, was indicted for attempting to help an al Qaeda operative enter the United States in order to attack gas stations. He was convicted in 2005.

- **Abdurahman Alamoudi.** *Abdurahman Alamoudi* (51), a naturalized U.S. citizen from Eritrea, was indicted in the United States for plotting to assassinate Saudi Arabia's Prince Abdullah.

- **Ahmed Omar Abu Ali.** *Ahmed Omar Abu Ali* (22), a native U.S. citizen, was arrested by Saudi authorities and later extradited to the United States for providing support to a terrorist organization and plotting to assassinate the president of the United States.

2004

- **Mohammed Abdullah Warsame.** *Mohammed Abdullah Warsame* (31), a legal permanent resident from Somalia, was arrested for conspiring to support al Qaeda. He was found guilty and sentenced in 2009.

- **Ilyas Ali.** *Ilyas Ali* (55), a naturalized U.S. citizen from India, pleaded guilty to providing material support to the Taliban and al Qaeda. He attempted to sell hashish and heroin in return for Stinger missiles, which he then planned to sell to the Taliban. Two other defendants, *Muhammed Abid Afridi* and *Syed Mustajab Shah*, both Pakistani nationals, were also convicted in the case.

- **Amir Abdul Rashid.** *Ryan Gibson Anderson* (26)—a native U.S. citizen and convert to Islam who called himself Amir Abdul Rashid—was a soldier in the U.S. Army at Fort Lewis, Washington, when he was arrested in February 2004 for contacting Islamic websites related to al Qaeda and offering information about the U.S. Army.

- **Mark Robert Walker.** A Wyoming Technical Institute student, *Mark Robert Walker* (19), a native U.S. citizen who, according to reports, became obsessed with jihad, was charged with attempting to assist the Somali-based group, Al-Ittihad al Islami. He planned to provide the group with night-vision devices and bulletproof vests.

- **Mohammed Junaid Babar.** *Mohammed Junaid Babar* (31), a naturalized U.S. citizen from Pakistan, was arrested in New York for providing material support to al Qaeda.

- **The Herald Square Plotters.** *Shahawar Martin Siraj* (22), a Pakistani national, and *James Elshafy* (19), a U.S.-born citizen, were arrested for plotting to carry out a terrorist attack on New York City's Herald Square subway station.

- **The Albany Plotters.** *Yassin Aref* (34), an Iraqi refugee in the United States, and *Mohammad Hossain* (49), a naturalized U.S. citizen from Bangladesh, two leaders of a mosque in Albany, New York, were arrested for attempting to acquire weapons in order to assassinate a Pakistani diplomat.

- **Adam Yahiye Gadahn.** *Adam Yahiye Gadahn* (26), a native U.S. citizen and convert to Islam, moved to Pakistan in 1998. By 2004, he was identified as a member of al Qaeda planning terrorist attacks in the United States, and he subsequently became one of al Qaeda's principal spokesmen. He was formally indicted in 2006.

- **The Abdi Case.** *Nuradin Abdi* (32), a Somali national granted asylum in the United States, was indicted in June 2004 for plotting with Iyman Faris to blow up a Columbus, Ohio, shopping mall. (He was arrested in November 2003.)

- **Gale Nettles.** *Gale Nettles* (66), a native U.S. citizen and ex-convict, was arrested in August in an FBI sting for plotting to bomb the Dirksen Federal Building in Chicago and for attempting to provide al Qaeda with explosive material. His motive was revenge for his conviction as a counterfeiter, but he wanted to connect with al Qaeda, which he figured would pay him for his excess explosive materials. He was convicted on the terrorist charge in 2005.

- **Carpenter and Ransom.** Two New Orleans men, *Cedric Carpenter* (31), a convicted felon, and *Lamont Ransom* (31), both native U.S. citizens, intended to sell fraudulent identity documents to the Philippine jihadist terrorist group Abu Sayyaf in return for cash and heroin. Ransom, who had previously served in the U.S. Navy, was familiar with the group. Both were convicted and sentenced in 2005.

2005

- **The New York Defendants.** Three defendants—*Mahmud Faruq Brent* (32), a U.S.-born citizen who had attended a training camp in Pakistan run by Lashkar-e-Toiba; *Rafiq Abdus Sabir* (50), a U.S.-born citizen and medical doctor who volunteered to provide medical treatment to al Qaeda terrorists; and *Abdulrahman Farhane* (52), a naturalized U.S. citizen from Morocco who agreed to assist in fundraising for the purchase of weapons for insurgents in Chechnya and Afghanistan—were linked to defendant-turned-informant *Tarik Shah* (42), a U.S.-born citizen who was arrested in May 2005 for offering to provide training to insurgents in Iraq. Shah identified his co-defendants, and all four were convicted.

- **The Lodi Case.** *Hamid Hayat* (22), a native-born U.S. citizen, and his father, *Umar Hayat*, a naturalized U.S. citizen from Pakistan, were arrested in June 2005 for secretly attending a terrorist training camp in Pakistan. Umar Hayat ultimately pleaded guilty of lying to federal authorities.

- **The Torrance Plotters.** *Kevin James* (29), *Levar Washington* (21), and *Gregory Patterson* (25), all native U.S. citizens and converts to Islam, and *Hammad Riaz Samana* (21), a permanent resident from Pakistan, were charged in August 2005 with planning to carry out terrorist attacks on National Guard armories, a U.S. military recruiting center, the Israeli consulate, and Los Angeles International airport. (This case is sometimes referred to as the Sacramento Plot.)

- **Michael Reynolds.** *Michael Reynolds* (47), a native U.S. citizen, acquired explosives and offered them to an informant whom he believed was an al Qaeda official to blow up the Alaska Pipeline in return for $40,000.

- **Ronald Grecula.** *Ronald Grecula* (70), a native U.S. citizen, was arrested in Texas in May 2005 for offering to build an explosive device for informants he believed to be al Qaeda agents. He pleaded guilty to the charge in 2006.

2006

- **The Liberty City Seven.** Seven men—*Narseal Batiste* (32), a native U.S. citizen; *Patrick Abraham* (39), a Haitian national illegally in the United States after overstaying his visa; *Stanley Grunt Phanor* (31), a naturalized U.S. citizen; *Naudimar Herrera* (22), a native U.S. citizen; *Burson Augustin* (21), a native U.S. citizen; *Rothschild Augustin* (26), a native U.S. citizen; and *Lyglenson Lemorin* (31), a legal permanent resident from Haiti—were charged in June 2006 with plotting to blow up the FBI building in Miami and the Sears Tower in Chicago. Herrera and Lemorin were acquitted.

- **Syed Hashmi.** *Syed "Fahad" Hashmi* (30), a Pakistani-born U.S. citizen, was arrested in London on charges of providing material support to al Qaeda.

- **Derrick Shareef.** *Derrick Shareef* (22), a native U.S. citizen and convert to Islam, was arrested for planning a suicide attack on an Illinois shopping mall. He intended to place hand grenades in garbage cans, but the plot also involved handguns.

- **The Fort Dix Plotters.** Six men—*Mohammad Ibrahim Shnewer* (22), a naturalized U.S. citizen from Jordan; *Serdar Tatar* (23), a legal permanent resident from Turkey; *Agron Abdullahu* (24), a U.S. permanent resident from Kosovo; and *Dritan Duka* (28), *Shain Duka* (26), and *Elljvir Duka* (23), three brothers from Albania living in the United States illegally—were charged with plotting to carry out an armed attack on soldiers at Fort Dix, New Jersey.

- **The Toledo Cluster.** *Mohammad Zaki Amawi* (26) and *Marwan El-Hindi* (43), both naturalized U.S. citizens from Jordan, and *Wassim Mazloum* (25), a legal permanent resident from Lebanon, were arrested in Toledo, Ohio, for plotting to build bombs to use against American forces in Iraq. Two additional persons were also charged in this case: *Zubair Ahmed* (26), a U.S.-born citizen, and his cousin *Khaleel Ahmed* (25), a naturalized U.S. citizen from India.

- **The Georgia Plotters.** *Syed Harris Ahmed* (21), a naturalized U.S. citizen, and *Ehsanul Islam Sadequee* (20), a U.S.-born citizen from Atlanta, Georgia, were arrested in April 2006 for discussing potential targets with terrorist organizations and receiving instruction in reconnaissance.

- **Daniel Maldonado.** *Daniel Maldonado* (27), a native U.S. citizen and convert to Islam, was arrested for joining a jihadist training camp in Somalia. He was captured by the Kenyan armed forces and returned to the United States.

- **Williams and Mirza.** Federal authorities charged two students at Houston Community College—*Kobie Diallo Williams* (33), a native U.S. citizen and convert to Islam, and *Adnan Babar Mirza* (29), a Pakistani national who had overstayed his student visa—with aiding the Taliban. According to the indictment, the two planned to join and train with the Taliban in order to fight U.S. forces in the Middle East.

- **Ruben Shumpert.** *Ruben Shumpert* (26), also known as Amir Abdul Muhaimin, a native U.S. citizen who had been convicted for drug trafficking, converted to Islam shortly after his release from prison. When the FBI came looking for him in 2006, he fled to Somalia and joined al-Shabaab. He was reportedly killed in Somalia in December 2008.

2007

- **Hassan Abujihaad.** *Hassan Abujihaad* (31), formerly known as Paul R. Hall, a native U.S. citizen and convert to Islam who had served in the U.S. Navy, was arrested in

April 2007 for giving the locations of U.S. naval vessels to an organization accused of supporting terrorists.

- **The JFK Airport Plotters.** *Russell Defreitas* (63), a naturalized U.S. citizen from Guyana; *Abdul Kadir* (55) a Guyanese citizen; *Kareem Ibrahim* (56), a Trinidadian; and *Abdal Nur* (57), another Guyanese citizen, were charged in June 2007 with plotting to blow up aviation fuel tanks at John F. Kennedy Airport in New York. Defreitas was arrested in Brooklyn. The other three plotters were arrested in Trinidad and extradited to the United States.

- **Ahmed Abdellatif Sherif Mohamed.** *Ahmed Abdellatif Sherif Mohamed* (26), a U.S. permanent resident from Egypt, was arrested for providing material support to terrorists by disseminating bomb-making instructions on YouTube. He pleaded guilty to the charge.

- **Omar Hammami.** Now known as Abu Mansour al-Amriki, *Omar Hammami* (23), a native-born U.S. citizen, left Alabama some time not later than 2007 to join al-Shabaab in Somalia. He later appeared in the group's recruiting videos. Hammami was indicted in 2010 for providing support to al-Shabaab.

- **Jaber Elbaneh.** *Jaber Elbaneh* (41), a naturalized U.S. citizen from Yemen, was convicted in absentia by a Yemeni court for plotting to attack oil and gas installations in Yemen. He had previously been charged in the United States with conspiring with the Lackawanna Six. He was one of a number of al Qaeda suspects who escaped from a Yemeni prison in 2006. He subsequently turned himself in to Yemeni authorities.

- **The Hamza Case.** Federal authorities charged the owner and several officials of Hamza, Inc., a financial institution, for money laundering and secretly providing money to al Qaeda. Those charged included *Saifullah Anjum Ranjha* (43), a legal permanent U.S. resident from Pakistan; *Imdad Ullah Ranjha* (32), also a legal permanent resident from Pakistan; and *Muhammed Riaz Saqi*, a Pakistani national living in Washington, D.C. Also charged in the case were three Pakistani nationals living in Canada and Spain.

2008

- **Christopher Paul.** *Christopher "Kenyatta" Paul* (43), a native U.S. citizen and convert to Islam living overseas, was arrested upon his return to the United States in April 2008 for having plotted terrorist attacks on various U.S. targets. He later pleaded guilty.

- **Bryant Vinas.** *Bryant Vinas* (26), a native U.S. citizen and convert to Islam, was arrested in Pakistan and extradited to the United States for having joined al Qaeda in Pakistan. He also provided al Qaeda with information to help plan a bombing attack on the Long Island Rail Road.

- **Somali Recruiting Case I.** As many as a dozen Somalis may have been recruited in the Minneapolis, Minnesota, area by *Shirwa Ahmed* (26), a naturalized U.S. citizen from Somalia, to fight in Somalia. Ahmed subsequently was killed in a suicide bombing in Somalia.

- **Sharif Mobley.** *Sharif Mobley* (26), a native U.S. citizen of Somali descent, moved to Yemen in 2008, ostensibly to study Arabic and religion, but in reality, authorities believe, to join a terrorist organization. He was later arrested by Yemeni authorities in a roundup of al Qaeda and al-Shabaab militants. In March 2010, he killed one guard and wounded another in an attempt to escape.

2009

- **The Riverdale Synagogue Plot.** Native U.S. citizens *James Cromite* (55), *David Williams* (28), *Onta Williams* (32), and *Laguerre Payen* (27), a Haitian national, all converts to Islam, were arrested in an FBI sting in New York in May 2009 for planning to blow up synagogues.

- **Abdulhakim Mujahid Muhammad.** In June 2009, *Abdulhakim Mujahid Muhammad* (23), also known as Carlos Bledsoe, a native U.S. citizen and Muslim convert, killed one soldier and wounded another at an Army recruiting station in Arkansas.

- **The North Carolina Cluster.** *Daniel Boyd* (39), a native U.S. citizen and convert to Islam who fought against the Soviets in Afghanistan in the late 1980s, was arrested in July 2009 along with his two sons, *Zakarlya Boyd* (20) and *Dylan Boyd* (22), also converts to Islam, and four others, including three U.S. citizens—*Anes Subasic* (33), a naturalized U.S. citizen from Bosnia; *Mohammad Omar Aly Hassan* (22), a U.S.-born citizen; and *Ziyad Yaghi* (21), a naturalized U.S. citizen—and *Hysen Sherifi* (24), a legal U.S. resident from Kosovo, for plotting terrorist attacks in the United States and abroad. *Jude Kenan Mohammad* (20), a U.S.-born citizen, was also a member of the group. He was arrested by Pakistani authorities in 2008. Boyd reportedly reconnoitered the Marine Corps base at Quantico, Virginia.

- **Betim Kaziu.** *Betim Kaziu* (21), a native U.S. citizen, was arrested in September 2009 for traveling overseas to join al-Shabaab or to attend a terrorist training camp in Somalia.

- **Ali Saleh Kahlah al-Marri.** *Ali Saleh Kahlah al-Marri* (38), a U.S. permanent resident and dual national of Qatar and Saudi Arabia, was charged with attending an al Qaeda training camp in Pakistan. He pleaded guilty to providing material support to a terrorist group.

- **Michael Finton.** *Michael Finton* (29), a native U.S. citizen and convert to Islam, was arrested in September 2009 in an FBI sting for planning to blow up a federal courthouse in Springfield, Illinois.

- **Hosam Maher Smadi.** *Hosam Maher Smadi* (19), a Jordanian citizen living in the United States, was arrested in September 2009 in an FBI sting for planning to blow up an office building in Dallas, Texas.

- **Najibullah Zazi.** *Najibullah Zazi* (25), a permanent U.S. resident from Afghanistan, was arrested in September 2009 for receiving training in explosives at a terrorist training camp in Pakistan and buying ingredients for explosives in preparation for a terrorist attack in the United States. Indicted with Zazi were his father, *Mohammed Zazi* (53), a naturalized U.S. citizen from Afghanistan, and *Ahmad Afzali* (38), a U.S. permanent resident from Afghanistan, both for making false statements to federal investigators; neither was involved in the terrorist plot. In January 2010, authorities arrested *Adis Medunjanin* (24), a naturalized U.S. citizen from Bosnia, and *Zarein Ahmedzay* (25), a naturalized U.S. citizen from Afghanistan, and charged them with participating in the plot.

- **Tarek Mehana.** In October 2009, federal authorities in Massachusetts arrested *Tarek Mehana* (27), a dual citizen of the United States and Egypt, for conspiring over a seven-year period to kill U.S. politicians, attack American troops in Iraq, and target shopping malls in the United States. Two other individuals, including *Ahmad Abousamra* (27), a U.S. citizen, were allegedly part of the conspiracy. Abousamra remains at large.

- **David Headley.** In an increasingly complicated case, *David Headley* (49), a U.S.-born citizen of Pakistani descent and resident of Chicago, was arrested in October 2009 along with *Tahawar Rana* (48), a native of Pakistan and a Canadian citizen, for planning terrorist attacks abroad. Headley was subsequently discovered to have participated in the reconnaissance of Mumbai prior to the November 2008 attack by the terrorist group Lashkar-e-Toiba. He pleaded guilty in March 2010.

- **Colleen Renee LaRose.** Calling herself "Jihad Jane" on the Internet, *Colleen Renee LaRose* (46), a native U.S. citizen and convert to Islam, was arrested in October 2009 for plotting to kill a Swedish artist whose drawings of Muhammad had enraged Muslims and for attempting to recruit others to terrorism. Her arrest was concealed until March 2010. LaRose pleaded guilty to the charges.

- **Nidal Hasan.** In November 2009, *Nidal Hasan* (38), a native U.S. citizen and Army major, opened fire on fellow soldiers at Fort Hood, Texas, killing 13 and wounding 31.

- **The Pakistan Five.** In November 2009, five Muslim Americans from Virginia— *Umar Farooq* (25), a naturalized U.S. citizen from Pakistan; *Ramy Zamzam* (22), who was born in Egypt, immigrated to the United States at the age of two, and became a citizen by virtue of his parents becoming citizens; *Waqar Hassan Khan* (22), a naturalized U.S. citizen from Pakistan; *Ahmad Abdullah Mimi* (20), a naturalized U.S. citizen from Eritrea; and *Aman Hassan Yemer* (18), a naturalized U.S. citizen from Ethiopia—were arrested in Pakistan for attempting to obtain training as jihadist guerrillas. Khalid Farooq, Umar Farooq's father, was also taken into custody but was later released. The five were charged by Pakistani authorities with planning terrorist attacks.

- **Somali Recruiting Case II.** In November 2009, federal authorities indicted eight men for recruiting at least 20 young men in Minnesota for jihad in Somalia and raising funds on behalf of al-Shabaab. By the end of 2009, a total of 14 indictments had been handed down as a result of the ongoing investigation. Those indicted, all but one of whom are Somalis, were *Abdow Munye Abdow,* a naturalized U.S. citizen from Somalia; *Khalid Abshir; Salah Osman Ahmad; Adarus Abdulle Ali; Cabdulaahi Ahmed Faarax; Kamal Hassan; Mohamed Hassan; Abdifatah Yusef Isse; Abdiweli Yassin Isse; Zakaria Maruf; Omer Abdi Mohamed,* a legal permanent resident from Somalia; *Ahmed Ali Omar; Mahanud Said Omar;* and *Mustafa Salat.* No age information is available.

- **Abdul Tawala Ibn Ali Alishtari.** *Abdul Tawala Ibn Ali Alishtari* (53), also known as Michael Mixon, a native U.S. citizen, was indicted and pleaded guilty to attempting to provide financing for terrorist training in Afghanistan.

2010[1]

- **Jamie Paulin-Ramirez.** The arrest of Colleen R. LaRose ("Jihad Jane") in 2009 led to further investigations and the indictment of *Jamie Paulin-Ramirez* (31), also known as "Jihad Jamie." Paulin-Ramirez, a native-born U.S. citizen and convert to Islam, allegedly accepted an invitation from LaRose to join her in Europe in order to attend a training camp there. According to the indictment, she flew to Europe with "the intent to live and train with jihadists." She was detained in Ireland and subsequently returned to the United States, where she was arraigned in April 2010.

- **Raja Lahrasib Khan.** *Raja Lahrasib Khan* (57), a naturalized U.S. citizen from Pakistan, was charged with sending money to Ilyas Kashmiri, an al Qaeda operative in Pakistan, and for discussing blowing up an unidentified stadium in the United States.

- **Times Square Bomber.** *Faisal Shazad* (30), a naturalized U.S. citizen from Pakistan, had studied and worked in the United States since 1999. In 2009, he traveled to Pakistan and contacted the TTP (Pakistan Taliban), who gave him instruction in bomb-building. Upon his return to the United States, he built a large incendiary device in a sport utility vehicle (SUV) and attempted unsuccessfully to detonate it in New York City's Times Square. He was arrested in May 2010. Three other individuals were arrested in the investigation but were never charged with criminal involvement in the case.

- **Wesam el-Hanafi and Sabirhan Hasanoff.** *Wesam el-Hanafi* (33), also known as "Khaled," a native-born U.S. citizen, and *Sabirhan Hasanoff* (34), also known as "Tareq," a dual U.S.-Australian citizen, were indicted for allegedly providing material

---

[1] In September 2010, Sami Samir Hassoun (22), was arrested in an FBI sting in Chicago for attempting to carry out a terrorist bombing. Hassoun expressed anger at Chicago Mayor Richard Daley. It is not clear that the case is jihadist-related. In December 2010, Awais Younis (26), a naturalized U.S. citizen from Afghanistan, was arrested for threatening to bomb the Washington, D.C., Metro system. He made the threat on Facebook, and it was reported to the authorities. Neither of these cases is included in the chronology.

support to a terrorist group. The two men, one of whom traveled to Yemen in 2008, provided al Qaeda with computer advice and assistance, along with other forms of aid.

- **Khalid Ouazzani.** *Khalid Ouazzani* (32) pleaded guilty in May to providing material support to a terrorist group. Ouazzani, a Moroccan-born U.S. citizen, admitted to raising money for al Qaeda through fraudulent loans, as well as performing other tasks at the request of the terrorist organization between 2007 and 2008.

- **Mohamed Mahmood Alessa and Carlos Eduardo Almonte.** Two New Jersey men, *Mohamed Mahmood Alessa* (20), a native U.S. citizen, and *Carlos Eduardo Almonte* (24), a naturalized citizen from the Dominican Republic and convert to Islam, were arrested in June at New York's JFK Airport for conspiring to kill persons outside the United States. The two were on their way to join al-Shabaab in Somalia.

- **Barry Walter Bujol, Jr.** *Barry Walter Bujol, Jr.* (29), a native U.S. citizen and convert to Islam, was arrested as he attempted to leave the United States to join al Qaeda in Yemen. He had been under investigation for two years and was in contact with an undercover agent he believed to be an al Qaeda operative.

- **Samir Khan.** In June 2010, the Yemen-based affiliate of al Qaeda began publishing *Inspire*, a slick, English-language online magazine devoted to recruiting Western youth to violent jihad. The man behind the new publication was *Samir Khan* (24), a Saudi-born naturalized U.S. citizen who moved to the United States with his parents when he was seven years old. He began his own journey to violent jihad when he was 15. He reportedly left the United States in late 2009, resurfacing in Yemen in 2010.

- **Rockwood's Hitlist.** *Paul Rockwood* (35), a U.S. citizen who served in the U.S. Navy and converted to Islam while living in Alaska, was convicted in July 2010 for lying to federal authorities about drawing up a list of 15 targets for assassination; they were targeted because, in his view, they offended Islam. He was also accused of researching how to build the explosive devices that would be used in the killings. His wife, *Nadia Rockwood* (36), who has dual UK-U.S. citizenship, was convicted of lying to authorities.

- **Zachary Chesser.** *Zachary Chesser* (20), a native U.S. citizen and convert to Islam, was arrested for supporting a terrorist group in July as he attempted to board an airplane to fly to Somalia and join al-Shabaab. Chesser had earlier threatened the creators of the television show *South Park* for insulting Islam in one of its episodes.

- **Shaker Masri.** A U.S. citizen by birth, *Shaker Masri* (26) was arrested in August 2010, allegedly just before he planned to depart for Afghanistan to join al Qaeda or Somalia to join al-Shabaab.

- **Somali Recruiting Case III.** As part of a continuing investigation of recruiting and funding for al Qaeda ally al-Shabaab, the U.S. Department of Justice announced four indictments charging 14 persons with providing money, personnel, and services to the terrorist organization. In Minnesota, 10 men were charged with terrorism offenses for leaving the United States to join al-Shabaab: *Ahmed Ali Omar* (27), a legal permanent resident; *Khalid Mohamud Abshir* (27); *Zakaria Maruf* (31), a legal permanent resident; *Mohamed Abdullahi Hassan* (22), a legal permanent resident; *Mustafa Ali Salat* (20), a legal permanent resident; *Cabdulaahi Ahmed Faarax* (33), a U.S. citizen; and *Abdiweli Yassin Isse* (26). Three were new on the list and had been the subject of previous indictments: *Abdikadir Ali Abdi* (19), a U.S. citizen; *Abdisalan Hussein Ali* (21), a U.S. citizen; and *Farah Mohamed Beledi* (26). A separate indictment named *Amina Farah Ali* (33) and *Hawo Mohamed Hassan* (63), both naturalized U.S. citizens, for fundraising on behalf of al-Shabaab. A fourth indictment charged *Omar Shafik Hammami* (26), a U.S. citizen from Alabama, and *Jehad Sherwan Mostafa* (28) of San Diego, California, with providing material support to al-Shabaab. (Hammami's involvement is listed in this chronology under the year 2007, when he first left the United States to join al-Shabaab; Mostafa is listed separately in the next entry.)

- **Jehad Serwan Mostafa.** In August 2010, *Jehad Serwan Mostafa* (28), a native U.S. citizen, was indicted for allegedly joining al-Shabaab in Somalia. He reportedly left the United States in December 2005 and was with al-Shabaab between March 2008 and June 2009.

- **Abdel Hameed Shehadeh.** *Abdel Hameed Shehadeh* (21), a U.S.-born citizen of Palestinian origin, was arrested in October for traveling to Pakistan to join the Taliban or another group to wage jihad against U.S. forces. Denied entry to Pakistan, then Jordan, Shehadeh returned to the United States and subsequently attempted to join the U.S. Army. He allegedly hoped to deploy to Iraq, where he planned to desert and join the insurgents. When that did not work out, he tried again to leave the country to join the Taliban.

- **Farooque Ahmed.** *Farooque Ahmed* (34), a naturalized U.S. citizen from Pakistan, was arrested in October for allegedly plotting to bomb Metro stations in Washington, D.C. FBI undercover agents learned of Ahmed's intentions by posing as al Qaeda operatives.

- **Shabaab Support Network in San Diego.** *Saeed Moalin* (33), a naturalized U.S. citizen from Somalia, *Mohamed Mohamed Mohamud* (38), born in Somalia, and *Issa Doreh* (54), a naturalized U.S. citizen from Somalia, all residents of San Diego, were arrested for allegedly providing material support to al-Shabaab. The investigation of this network is continuing, and a fourth man from Southern California, *Ahmed Nasir Taalil Mohamud* (35), was subsequently indicted.

- **Al-Shabaab Fundraising II.** In November, federal authorities arrested *Mohamud Abdi Yusuf* (24), a St. Louis resident, and *Abdi Mahdi Hussein* (35) of Minneapolis, both immigrants from Somalia. The two are accused of sending money to al-Shabaab in Somalia. A third person, *Duane Mohamed Diriye*, believed to be in Africa, was also indicted.

- **Nima Ali Yusuf.** *Nima Ali Yusuf* (24), a legal permanent resident originally from Somalia, was arrested in November for allegedly providing material support to a terrorist group. She was accused of attempting to recruit fighters and raise funds for al-Shabaab.

- **Mohamed Osman Mohamud.** *Mohamed Osman Mohamud* (19), a naturalized U.S. citizen originally from Somalia, was arrested in December for attempting to detonate what he believed to be a truck bomb at an outdoor Christmas-tree-lighting ceremony in Portland, Oregon. He reportedly had wanted to carry out some act of violent jihad since the age of 15. His bomb was, in fact, an inert device given to him by the FBI, which set up the sting after it became aware of his extremism through a tip and subsequent monitoring of his correspondence on the Internet.

- **Antonio Martinez.** *Antonio Martinez* (21), also known as Muhaamed Hussain, a naturalized U.S. citizen and convert to Islam, was arrested in December for allegedly plotting to blow up the Armed Forces Career Center in Catonsville, Maryland. The car bomb he used to carry out the attack was a fake device provided to him by the FBI, which had been communicating with him for two months.

Bibliography

Abu-Nasr, Donna, and Lee Keath, "200 Websites Spread Al-Qaida's Message in English: Increasing Numbers of Radical Islamic Websites Are Spreading al-Qaida's Message in English," The Associated Press, November 14, 2009.

Bakker, Edwin, Presentation at the International Security Forum 2011, Zurich, Switzerland, May 31, 2011.

Bjorgo, Tore, and John Horgan (eds.), *Leaving Terrorism Behind: Individual and Collective Disengagement*, Abingdon, UK: Routledge, 2009.

Bush, George W., *Decision Points,* New York: Crown Publishers, 2010.

The Center on Law and Security, NYU School of Law, *The NYU Review of Law & Security, The Bulletin on Law & Security,* and other publications, New York: New York University. As of July 25, 2011: http://www.lawandsecurity.org

———, *Terrorist Trial Report Card Update April 2011*, New York: New York University, 2011.

Clapper, James R., Statement for the Record on the Worldwide Threat Assessment of the U.S. Intelligence Community for the House Permanent Select Committee on Intelligence, Office of the Director of National Intelligence, February 10, 2011.

CNN, "Purported al-Awlaki Message Calls for Jihad Against U.S.," March 17, 2010. As of April 12, 2010: http://news.blogs.cnn.com/2010/03/17/purported-al-awlaki-message-calls-for-jihad-against-u-s/

Cragin, Kim, *Understanding Terrorist Motivations*, Testimony presented before the House Homeland Security Committee, Subcommittee on Intelligence, Information Sharing and Terrorism Risk Assessment on December 15, 2009, Santa Monica, Calif.: RAND Corporation, CT-338, 2009. As of April 9, 2010: http://www.rand.org/pubs/testimonies/CT338.html

Dolnick, Sam, "U.S. Registry Ends, but Not Fallout," *International Herald Tribune*, June 1, 2011.

Elliott, Andrea, "The Jihadist Next Door," *The New York Times Magazine*, January 31, 2010.

Europol, *TE-SAT 2011: EU Terrorism and Trend Report*, 2011. As of August 4, 2011: https://www.europol.europa.eu/latest_publications/2/2011

Eoropol, *Europol Report 2009*, 2010. As of August 4, 2011: https://www.europol.europa.eu/latest_publications/2/2010

"Fact Checking the Sunday Shows—March 6, 2011," MediaMatters Action Network, March 7, 2011.

Gartenstein-Ross, Daveed, and Laura Grossman, *Homegrown Terrorists in the U.S. and U.K.: An Empirical Examination of the Radicalization Process*, Washington, D.C.: FDD Press, 2009. As of April 9, 2010: http://www.defenddemocracy.org/downloads/HomegrownTerrorists_USandUK.pdf

Greenberg, Karen J., "Homegrown: The Rise of American Jihad," *The New Republic*, May 21, 2010. As of July 25, 2011: http://www.tnr.com//article/75075/homegrown

Hannah, Greg, Lindsay Clutterbuck, and Jennifer Rubin, *Radicalization or Rehabilitation: Understanding the Challenge of Extremist and Radicalized Prisoners*, Santa Monica, Calif.: RAND Corporation, TR-571-RC, 2008. As of April 9, 2010: http://www.rand.org/pubs/technical_reports/TR571.html

Horgan, John, *Walking Away from Terrorism: Accounts of Disengagement from Radical and Extremist Movements*, Abingdon, UK: Routledge, 2009.

Horowitz, Craig, "Anatomy of a Foiled Plot," *New York*, May 21, 2005.

Humaidan, M. D., "Scholar Warns Against Al-Qaeda's Recruitment of Youth via Internet," *Arab News,* January 15, 2011, citing a study by Colonel Faiz Al-Shihri. As of July 24, 2011: http://arabnews.com/saudiarabia/article234730.ece

Jacobson, Michael, *Terrorist Dropouts: Learning from Those Who Have Left*, Washington, D.C.: The Washington Institute for Near East Policy, January 2010.

Jenkins, Brian Michael, *Terrorism in the United States*, Santa Monica, Calif.: RAND Corporation, P-6474, 1980. As of April 9, 2010: http://www.rand.org/pubs/papers/P6474.html

———, *Building an Army of Believers: Jihadist Radicalization and Recruitment*, Testimony presented before the House Homeland Security Committee, Subcommittee on Intelligence, Information Sharing and Terrorism Risk Assessment on April 5, 2007, Santa Monica, Calif.: RAND Corporation, CT-278-1, 2007a. As of April 9, 2010: http://www.rand.org/pubs/testimonies/CT278-1.html

———, *Defining the Role of a National Commission on the Prevention of Violent Radicalization and Homegrown Terrorism*, Testimony presented before the House Committee on Homeland Security, Subcommittee on Intelligence, Information Sharing, and Terrorism Risk Assessment on June 14, 2007, Santa Monica, Calif.: RAND Corporation, CT-285, 2007b. As of April 9, 2010: http://www.rand.org/pubs/testimonies/CT285.html

———, *Going Jihad: The Fort Hood Slayings and Home-Grown Terrorism*, Testimony presented before the Senate Homeland Security and Governmental Affairs Committee on November 19, 2009, Santa Monica, Calif.: RAND Corporation, CT-336, 2009. As of April 9, 2010: http://www.rand.org/pubs/testimonies/CT336.html

———, *Would-Be Warriors: Incidents of Jihadist Terrorist Radicalization in the United States Since September 11, 2001*, Santa Monica, Calif.: RAND Corporation, OP-292-RC, 2010. As of August 4, 2011: http://www.rand.org/pubs/occasional_papers/OP292.html

Khatchadourian, Raffi, "Azzam the American: The Making of an Al Qaeda Homegrown," *The New Yorker*, January 22, 2007.

Kurzman, Charles, *The Missing Martyrs: Why There Are So Few Muslim Terrorists*, Oxford, UK: Oxford University Press, 2011.

Leiter, Michael E., Testimony before the U.S. House of Representatives Committee on Homeland Security, Washington, D.C., February 9, 2011.

McCauley, Clark, and Sophia Moskalenko, "Mechanisms of Radicalization: Pathways Toward Terrorism," *Terrorism and Political Violence*, Vol. 20, 2008.

Moss, Michael, and Souad Mekhennet, "An Internet Jihad Aims at U.S. Viewers," *The New York Times*, October 15, 2007.

Napolitano, Janet, Testimony before the U.S. House of Representatives Committee on Homeland Security, "Understanding the Homeland Threat Landscape—Considerations for the 112th Congress," Washington, D.C., February 9, 2011.

The NEFA Foundation, *Anwar al Awlaki: Pro Al-Qaida Ideologue with Influence in the West*, February 5, 2009. As of April 9, 2010: http://www.nefafoundation.org/miscellaneous/FeaturedDocs/nefabackgrounder_alawlaki.pdf

Pew Research Center, *Muslim Americans: Middle Class and Mostly Mainstream*, Washington, D.C., May 22, 2007.

Pipes, Daniel, "Which Has More Islamist Terrorism, Europe or America?" *Jerusalem Post*, July 3, 2008. As of July 25, 2011: http://www.danielpipes.org/5723/which-has-more-islamist-terrorism-europe-or-america

Roy, Olivier, "Radicalisation and Deradicalisation," in International Centre for the Study of Radicalisation (ICSR), *Perspectives on Radicalization and Political Violence: Papers from the First International Conference on Radicalisation and Political Violence,* March 2008.

Sageman, Marc, *Leaderless Jihad: Terror Networks in the Twenty-First Century,* Philadelphia, Pa.: University of Pennsylvania Press, 2008.

————, *Understanding Terror Networks,* Philadelphia, Pa.: University of Pennsylvania Press, 2004.

Schanzer, David, Charles Kurzman, and Ebrahim Moosa, *Anti-Terror Lessons of Muslim Americans,* Durham, N.C.: Duke University, January 6, 2010.

Silber, Mitchell D., and Arvin Bhatt, *Radicalization in the West: The Homegrown Threat,* New York: New York City Police Department, 2007.

Tempest, Rone, "In Lodi Terror Case, Intent Was the Clincher," *Los Angeles Times,* May 1, 2006.

Temple-Raston, Dina, *The Jihad Next Door: The Lackawanna Six and Rough Justice in an Age of Terror,* New York: PublicAffairs Books, 2007.

Valla, Edward J., and Gregory Comcowich, "Domestic Terrorism: Forgotten, but Not Gone," in Jeffrey N. Norwitz (ed.), *Armed Groups: Studies in National Security, Counterterrorism, and Counterinsurgency,* Newport, R.I.: U.S. Naval War College, 2008.

Vidino, Lorenzo, "Homegrown Jihadist Terrorism in the United States: A New and Occasional Phenomenon," *Studies in Conflict & Terrorism,* Vol. 32, No. 1, 2009.

————, *Radicalization, Linkage, and Diversity: Current Trends in Terrorism in Europe,* Santa Monica, Calif.: RAND Corporation, OP-333-OSD, 2011. As of July 25, 2011:
http://www.rand.org/pubs/occasional_papers/OP333.html

Weinmann, Gabriel, *Terror on the Internet: The New Arena, the New Challenges,* Washington, D.C.: United States Institute for Peace, 2006.